IRON

OF THE

SKY

BY

RYAN DOWNEY

Iron Of The Sky

Ryan Downey

ISBN (Print Edition): 978-1-54398-832-1

ISBN (eBook Edition): 978-1-54398-833-8

Special Thanks To My Editors:

Rita Mermaid, J-Dizzle (aka Professor Manhands), Bee,
SO (aka The Kid), El Jefe, Sneeze, Newbie, Delco Joe
Moranis Goldblum, Mikeropenis Ramrod, Varga Girl,
Kane Man, Gatorade, Red Jimmy, The Indian, M&Ms,
Doc, Heather Reformed, Ask Alexa, and No Merce E

Cover Art By Allie Osipov

Additional assistance/information provided by: Jessica Kline,
Tim McGee (Bonner '07), Elisabetta "Lulu" Spadafora,
Ryan Rathfon, Erika Rathfon, Hillary Paige Stockard

And Sylvester Stallone via Rocky "The Italian Stallion" Balboa
For always reminding me that it's not about how hard you hit

To The Sunbathers, Stargazers, Moon
Dancers And World Changers

Enjoy all of life's little romances

And To Niki

Keep Looking Up

PROLOGUE

It was common in those days to believe that the sky, like everything else, was controlled by the gods. That anything seen that could not be explained by their version of modern science, must be a sign from the heavens. Some of these signs were taken to be omens, warnings that man was in big trouble with its celestial parents. Death from above. A comet brought pestilence in the whip of its tail. An eclipse was god turning blind eye to a flood. Meteor showers turned king against king. Brother against brother. These people worshipped Ra, among others, for the same reasons anyone worships; fear and desperation.

On a night as any other the newly appointed king sat idly in his throne with nothing to do. His age was of little consequence to those who feared him as were his noticeable defects, necrosis, scoliosis, and so on. A yawn past his overbite nearly turned whistle through cleft palate. As he readied himself to retire for the evening, a subject armed with the painfully boring task of standing guard on the balcony adjacent to the throne room came running in to inform the young king of what his tired eyes beheld.

He gazed upon Khonsu, god of the night sky. Glowing full and bright, Khonsu, who had come to prominence in this particular dynasty, was armed with the all too important task of slaying the king's enemies. In His travels He kept careful time for a people who would rule for centuries. And at some point or another He may or may not have created the universe.

So entranced by his protector the king could barely hear what his foolish subject was prattling on about. It seems one of the stars had fallen from the sky and fearing it may be portent, the young king felt it warranted immediate tending. The spotter was sent of course, along with several other well-suited footmen. Patriots to a nation who charted the stars for millennia and built a map to them here on earth, their mission was simple and duty clear. Return the star to heaven.

Late in winter, the stars had already been sticking around for dawn. The hours of the night were fixed, the land riddled with landmarks and the star that ditched the constellation party early was easily found in less than a week. Their horses would get little rest as their find was a great gift that would certainly please the king. The Egyptians were experts at moving huge rocks and the horse would serve as good a slave as any.

His majesty was in the middle of a game of senet when they reached the gates. His opponent was letting him win when they entered the court to tell the king the good news. Their journey had taken less than a full day's time and while several were wary that the find was a bad omen, the rest were simply pleased because he was pleased.

Kings have no use for a dusty old space rock sitting around so his subjects set to breaking it up further (unbeknownst to the king most of it still lay where they found it) to mine the interstellar ore. With the Bronze Age coming to a close and a new age dawning, they had become pretty handy with metals, precious or otherwise. They were to each craft something special. Something unique. Which of course meant the king was going to get a succession of useless trinkets, bowls and goblets that made food and beverage taste funny, and scepters a fraction of the size of the one he already wielded. The pharaoh was gracious enough to yawn his way through the parade of disappointments. Brushing the last of the insults aside, the young man up and left for the great dining hall for dinner.

In the food preparation area, the cook was feverishly finishing his particular craft. He probably should have been more nervous than he was, it was a dish he'd never prepared prior. The fish was an unfamiliar species. Most were for people who rarely ate fish living on the world's second largest river. People who worshipped half the animals on the land. And a people who farmed in a land arid on its best day and prone to drought, famine, flooding, and locust. Still they maintained a primarily vegetarian diet and a strange and decadent fish would not suffice alone, no matter how well smoked and seasoned.

Accompanying the fish that would go relatively untouched was a vegetable barley soup, the chef's specialty, and honey bread cakes, the king's personal favorite. And there was the usual assortment of nuts, dates and figs, olives, a fragrant mélange, exotic candies, and a myriad of rare delicacies no peasant would ever taste.

Much like most kids his age, he could really pack it in. He sat completely stuffed on the terrace following his lavish banquet. Two harpists and a double oboist comprised the band set to be entertaining him as he let out exhaust into the chill of the night air. Shifting in his seat, he contemplated all possible reasons why his breath was now visible, figuring it was merely demons being exhumed thanks to divine intervention. A man appeared in the doorway and begged the guards to allow him audience. The king looked up wistfully and waved his fingers casually to let him pass. The guards were substantially more nonplussed and nearly tackled the man when he removed his offering. Desperate not to be impaled, he assured them he meant His Majesty no earthly harm, but had taken a tad longer to finish than the evening's earlier presenters. Convinced in his sincerity and aware of his history of loyal servitude, the king allowed him to step forward and received the gift. Darkness would not hide it once unsheathed as it caught the light of the moon and recast it on the spectators. Quite taken, the king did more than nod him aside. Special favor was taken upon the gift and the metal worker graciously thanked and rewarded. He would treasure it always.

Always would last nine more years. Less than a decade later and the boy who would be king became the slightly older boy who would be dead. While out in battle, clutching his favored gift which now lay on a nearby nightstand, his horse got tripped up, toppling his chariot, and fracturing the pharaoh's leg. A fractured leg was entirely too complex a condition for their version of modern medicine. Within a few hours he would be riding Ra's chariot to be united with Osiris and Thoth in A'aru, the Field Of Reeds. At the age of 19, he had lived more than halfway to his life expectancy. Not bad for an Egyptian. Once mummified, he would be buried in one of the few tombs in all the land not to be completely consumed by the sands of the Sahara, alongside his most prized possessions and beloved living servants.

Now at the mercy of the elements, their race to be discovered would be up against more than just sun, wind, and rain. What binds all things is not death. But decay. All things fall apart and deteriorate. Rot away, rust up, get eaten, break down, or erode. Recycling down to nothing. Lead is the final stage. Then of course there is the long-standing tradition of the natural enemy.

It wouldn't be long before his successors, discontented with changes implemented during his dynasty and throughout his reign would do their damnedest to eradicate all evidence that he and his family had ever existed. His influence reversed and name fell silent. But critics be cursed and archeologists be praised, damnatio memoriae would be no match for the innate quest for knowledge and the unending search for truth in a seemingly infinite universe.

PART I

Knocking Up

The woman upstairs didn't stir. The knock at the door didn't wake her. Neither did the doorbell. He was wide-awake in his recliner. The recliner no one else could sit in. The one directly in front of the television, obscuring some of the other views in the room. The knock only confused him. The neighbors would occasionally let him know when the TV got too loud. It was Saturday Night At The Movies and Channel 6 was playing Raiders, which meant the volume was cranked. Every crack of the whip was so sharp, it felt like old Indy was using it to swat flies off his ear lobes.

Thumb pressed firmly on the down arrow, the volume returned to a level that made each thwack of punch landed on Nazi face far less exhilarating as he anxiously awaited further indignant raps. When none came he began the slow crawl to what, at least he would deem, reasonable level. Until the ding-dong. Clear now that he had a visitor he glanced up the stairs to spy any signs of life and finding none ran to descend the staircase leading to the front door as to avoid another awakening ring. He held his breath all the way down.

First door open, visitor revealed, sigh of relief exhaled. He hadn't seen her in several weeks. Maybe closer to a month or two. Far too long regardless, a good hug and kiss of cheek would bring them back. As she began to ask him how he was doing, blaring cop sirens resounded. She made a scared face that always made him laugh. "They finally found you?" she implored and he laughed even harder. "Don't worry, I have a disguise," he assured and put a finger mustache to his upper lip. Her laugh was drowned out by the ever-growing intensity, then thanks to the Doppler Effect, they had to wait even longer after it passed. The cops caused the woman upstairs, Gillian, 26, hot, no last name given or warranted, to stir, but sleep maintained. He had by now forgotten all about her. The small talk didn't last for even if she hadn't showed up to his house in the middle of the night, he would be able to quickly discern that she had something to tell him.

"Alright, out with it," he commanded. "What say you who arouses me from my slumber at this ungodly hour?" Her distraction by lightning bug, Phontinus Pyralis, broke. "You weren't sleeping, shut up." He was defeated. "Well," she began collecting her thoughts. "I think I finally realized what bothers me so much about people who believe in astrology." Smiling, the struggle to not say anything began for him. "Oh?" He could allow himself one little word. "It isn't that it's completely arbitrary. Which it is." That modifier lit his eyes. Big as a weather balloon, if his pride continued swelling exponentially, he would bust. Always so reluctant to follow his lead, even when she knew he was… onto something. The iconoclast had trashed the pseudo-religion so many years ago and she had only ever half agreed with him.

"It's not how horoscopes are vague and interchangeable." He had heard people quote him, to him, many times over the years without the quoter quite knowing it was he they were reciting. But never so satisfyingly. "Or how the stars in the Zodiacs are nowhere near one another thus making the very idea moronic."

A laugh escaped. Surely she had practiced in the mirror before leaving the house. Which reminded him. "Say, where is uh-." "Oh, I wasn't going to wake him for this." He hadn't seen her without him in some time. Then, with no beat missed, "It's that it clearly illustrates how painfully un-self-aware people are. They're so oblivious. Most people already believe themselves to be generally good people. Which they're not." He could cry. "The hypocrisy compounds when on top of that they add exaggerated qualities of traits that they either possess minimally or not at all."

And there it was. His mouth agape. She gave him the answer he'd always looked for but never reached. The joy and pride almost distracted him from the fact that he knew that wasn't it. "Very good," he said in a calm hesitant voice. Then he waited until her face fell a bit. "And."

"And I'm getting married." "There it is," he exclaimed putting her into a bear hug. The elongation of embrace served purpose twofold. Time was needed to suppress tears fighting for freedom. And, like him, she didn't seem to want to let go. She had no tears to hide. Hers escaped on the walk over.

The release brought a mutual gaze that said all there was to be said between them. Both fluent in unspoken conversation.

A few cars drove by, one of the drivers honking thinking he was funny. A couple walking their dog, a golden retriever, forced him to take a step forward and while normally he would jump at the chance to make a furry friend, he let Gaia pass by unpetted. Before offering sincere congratulations, his gaze turned if ever briefly, to the sky. Searching for a recognizable cluster of stars, something tangible and familiar. Finding none, he turned back to her so as not to let the moment grow awkward. He had missed his chance and found himself lost in the city lights with nothing to hold onto, but a few sweet memories and the heart of a love lost so very long ago.

Familiar Landscapes

There was no wine for dinner. She grabbed her cloth shopping bag with the tropical fish and sea turtles on it and bolted out the back door. Passing down the narrow alley between her neighbors' houses. She could hear the clunky old mower had finally started up. Standing on tipped toes with hands keeping balance on top rail of the chained link fence she strained to see the mower at work. No such luck. If there was anything to be seen, she was the one to catch it. The girl with glasses far too big for her face gave up and scurried down the alley hopping puddles and dodging trashcans.

They were heavy, those glasses, and the bounce in her step would often jostle them loose, prompting a quick finger push to reset. The warm spring air felt good on her sensitive skin and she did her best to not let the rebirth of flora upset her allergies.

The elderly gentleman who ran the local liquor store welcomed her as always with an inviting smile. In the neighborhood forever, he was one of those guys who knew everyone. "What do you say, Miss? His glasses rested firmly on his nose as he checked inventory and as she fixed hers. "Having company tonight, Charlie," she beckoned from the aisle of whites. "The Chesters?" He even knew their friends. "No, they're out of town. Early vacation. The Ripleys." "Ah," he nodded and went back to his checklist. She huffed as she lifted a large bottle of Sauvignon Blanc by means of scrawny arm before heading to the aisle of reds. Then, upon choosing a Cab that hailed from the same vineyard, made her way to the counter.

"Will that be all, sweetheart?" he asked ringing her up quickly. "Yes, Charlie," she said with a smile. She was very fond of his nickname for her. He put the bottles in her bag from home and she paid cash, of course.

Her walk home was narrated by cicadas making their return. She thought of sweet, old Charlie and how she wasn't even sure if that was his first name. She didn't know his full name and whenever he introduced himself he'd always add "like the horse," then make a silly face. An introduction that incited an immediate liking to him.

Terror struck and thoughts of Charlie vanished. In an instant she found herself running on the street where she lived. She was cleverly illusive though, heading down side streets, she knew to head in the general direction rather than lead them straight there. "Look who bought us booze," was the last thing she heard before her feet were taking her faster than she thought she could go.

The bottles kept clanking against one another and a second fear arose thinking they may break. Pulling them up and wrapping them tight, she pressed them firm against her undeveloped chest and for once was glad she didn't have boobs. Managing to get a hand free, she took her glasses off. For the most part she knew the layout of the terrain and even though she was blind as a bat without them, she was dead in the water if they fell off and got lost again. The lucky rabbit was gaining ground as obnoxious taunts like "stupid bitch" were becoming progressively distant. An odd insult as she was neither.

Cutting through Mrs. Hobbs backyard, she burst through a gate, ripping her shirt, but taking her straight to a gravel road that ran between houses. Fast as she could, she spun, ducking behind the O'Reillys' garden shed and buried herself behind a wheel barrow. There she stayed until the stampede of trampling hooves faded and she caught her breath. "Shit." Those jerkoffs cost her one of her favorite shirts. The one with pink butterflies she had bought herself at the mall with babysitting money. With her glasses back on, she followed the gravel road to the main street and made her way home.

Going through the back door to the kitchen she placed the bottles on the table and put the bag back on top of the fridge. She reexamined the damage done to butterflies and deliberated if it was salvageable. Removing the wine key from the drawer next to the sink she opened both red and white. It had been offered to her many times, but she had always declined. She poured halfway to the top of a red solo cup and cheersed herself. To a most daring escape. As the Sauvé Blanc calmed her nerves and settled her mind, she could once again hear that mower. That rusted collection of clunky bolts and blades. Mind settled, she pondered what it was exactly that made that lawn one yard up and three yards over grow faster than all others.

Irish Goodbye

She found him. Not the other way around. It was customary practice for high school boys to chase baby bunnies like hound dogs on a track. And while he had pursued a great many already in his few years, on this day a surprise happened by.

He didn't have much money. Most teenagers don't. Landscaping is not going to make anyone rich, unless they own the company. And even then. But he spent summers making relatively decent wage working for a business owner whose company would go under before the young landscaper would graduate college. His anal, obsessive-compulsive leanings made him a valuable asset to his employer and a total pain in the ass to everyone else. Order of the day was a daunting one. Three properties in the same development and to fit them in meant a 6:00 AM call time. Hours of meticulous hedging and scrupulous clipping. The last thing a teenager wants to do once he makes it to Friday night is to be in bed in time to get up at cockcrow on Saturday. And like a good teenager, he wasn't. The woods weren't going to drink in themselves.

Alcoholics who had yet to tap their full potential, they hadn't finished all the hooch. There was still the majority of a case and collectively three full bottles under leaves and twigs by a marked tree. The house party wasn't until later and he was done work by late afternoon. The boys were waiting for him and just as rum fueled pirates to uncover buried treasure, state law led minors to buried rum.

The bottles were almost gone when he arrived. Just as well. He hadn't developed taste for it. A small fire blazed as he cracked his first beer. Between sips he would indulge in a swig or two of the hard stuff, but two nights in a row and a hard day's in between was more than enough incentive to pace himself.

Beer gone and bottles condensed to one, Dankar, an exchange student eager to fit in despite the school year being long over, shoved the bottle in his pants. They peed out the fire and these knuckleheads were on their way to an even grander ritual. The journey across town was arduous, given the sudden lack of consumption and waning buzz. They feared not.

Sted Burman was Master Of The House Party, Keeper Of The Inebriated, and tonight was Vulcanalia. The lush overgrowth diminished any clear visibility of the festivities taking place, but upon approach one could make out the glow of bonfire. The Crandalls were out of town and Sted was tending to responsibilities of being a good host with such fervor as to ensure it may be of no trouble to Martin Crandall whatsoever. So efficient was he, in fact, that Martin Crandall didn't even realize there was going to be a party until the keg was rolling up his driveway earlier that afternoon. Sted considered it no problem at all and was all too happy to oblige.

They entered the front door without knocking and Dankar cut straight for the kitchen to add the stash from his pants to the potluck of swag ravaged from older siblings, parents' liquor cabinets, and church tabernacle. He followed Dankar at a casual distance and grabbed a light beer from the fridge.

A Beirut tournament raged on in the dining room, he figured he could get in on it later. He soon found himself wandering, exploring the labyrinth of hall and den. A large TV in the basement was running *Animal House* on loop until the ever-prudish Susie Nguyan complained of how debaucherous it was and demanded it be changed. Tim Hutch jumped up and grabbed a copy of *Caddyshack*, which she had never seen either, and convinced her a lighthearted comedy about golf was far tamer.

There was a game he didn't recognize in the corner, much like pong, but with the entire table filled with cups. They were jokingly calling it 'Bubba Gump' because the creator claimed it would make anyone who played "retarded." Desiring to neither watch *Caddyshack* again nor to 'get retarded,' he ascended the back cement stairs that led through the Bilco double latch metal doors to the back patio and emerged in Crandall's backyard like a football player returning from the locker room.

The pit was not the only fire going out back, there were several throughout the immense acreage. Some were smoking up, some were burning whatever they could get their hands on; some were burning their hands as they were burning anything. Heathens blowing out the end of summer with spectacular antediluvian style and all taking part. All except he.

Left alone by so-called friends, ostracized by social cliques, in a backyard not his own, he felt the slightly overgrown grass beneath his shoes bouncing like a sponge. Adam O'Leary and Cole Myer were smoking on the patio. He didn't smoke himself, but secondhand never bothered him. Others sat around the nearby fire pit, source of their lit cigs. After imbibing gifted nicotine and tar for a moment he started walking towards the pines that ran along the property line with no discernable destination other than to leave.

King Of The Irish Goodbye, he cut between two Leyland Cypresses without a single word, one beer in hand and two in pocket. Having no baby, they were both for the road.

Crossing to the cattycorner block, he noticed a figure lingering near the intersection. Long hair made him guess the shadowy figure female; she appeared to be heading to the party, but at a gradual pace. Almost as if she had no intention of getting there. Paying her no mind, he turned back to his route and spotted a pair of headlights way up at the top of the street as he heard someone yell "wait" directly behind him. She had crossed the street and was scurrying to catch up with him. Her hair flapped this way and that. Before he could figure it out, she was standing directly in front of him. "Oh hey," he recognized her immediately. Can't forget a pair of glasses like those. "You were in my Bio and Pre-Calc, right?" She had been in a few of his classes over the years and she was, as he and everyone else remembered, the one kind enough to remind forgetful teachers if homework went unassigned. He minded far less than some, barely to the point past an eye roll, but it certainly granted no favor for her with their fellow peers. "On your way to Crandall's?" he asked. "Uh-huh," she lied leaving out the part where she wasn't invited and was only passing for a quick spy. "Ah. I got bored and decided to head out," he responded. As he conveniently left out the part where he was there primarily by association. The first set of headlights grew close enough to decipher make and model, with a second just like it coming up the rear. Paddy wagons barreled past them and whipped around the corner. "Time to go," he grabbed her hand and took off running down the block, not waiting to see the commotion that followed and not realizing she was perfectly capable of running without his help.

A considerable distance away, several blocks up and a few blocks over, they stood at the base of a bridge that carried car over creek. They came around to the side of the bridge to lurk in shadow in case any catchers sped by, nets grasped, looking for strays. Finishing the beer in hand, he broke out the other two and was gentleman enough to give her the now shaken back up. Lifting the tab as gently as they could and without losing hardly any through hissing foam, the familiar crack pierced the night's silence. Frogs hidden somewhere in the creek bed were the only to respond.

He raised a light beer most wouldn't use to wash crud off their tires and searched for an acceptable toast. "Here's to a… uh…" "A daring escape," she jumped in. He nodded in approval and their cans clinked. A siren kicked up and they instinctively ducked under the bridge. They couldn't tell how close it was and it didn't matter. She hadn't experienced this much excitement in at least a week and he certainly wasn't bored anymore. He looked up and around the base of the bridge to see if he could make anything out. She looked down. Her hand was being held again. Once more she resisted the urge to point out she needed no help hiding under a bridge. When he turned back, her face told him all he needed to know and not wanting to let the moment slip, without a single word, he kissed her.

"You sure know how to party, Sweetheart," he said once his tongue was freed. Cheek blushed and smile spread. "I have a friend who calls me that." "That right?" he responded, turning once more to make sure the coast was clear.

"Hope he doesn't mind if I borrow it." She did nothing to hide her ebullience; couldn't have even if she so desired. He did nothing to loosen his grip. "He won't mind." "Good," he said assuredly. "Now let's get the hell out of here." And he walked her home at a very considerable pace.

Aftershock

The unofficial end of summer was three weeks past and it was feeling more apparent by the day. But she refused to close her window. To save energy, the heat wasn't on yet and the chimney had yet to be cleaned. She had heard the ruptured evening air with that all too familiar struggle. Several rips of the cord and the little gas powered Black and Decker that could sputtered a healthy cloud of exhaust as the partially rusted blades began to spin. Less than a week left in the month, one yard back and three over, she never could quite see the cord ripper. She had always assumed, perhaps unfairly, that it was a young male. Maybe he was cute. Now she knew. He was. And he was hers. And the future was in their hands.

Imagination ran uncharacteristically wild as she desperately tried to avoid getting back to her Calculus. For the most part she had been raised conservatively and would think and dress as such. But hormones coursing though a developing body and the attention span of the average American teenager are two forces of nature that suffer no reckoning. With nurture effectively vanquished, her mind was free to carry out fantasy.

When she was finished, her problem remained before she could go downstairs for an early supper. Distance between two points should be easy enough.

$$2\Pi R/2Re = 38880/107 = 363.36\ldots$$

The numbers all seemed to run together.

$$3.844\,02 \times 108$$

Whatever. It was quarter past 4. She was distracted. And hungry. So it would just have to wait.

$$64\ 1/6\ R$$

Numerical nonsense. She would never get into AU at this rate. Not the best way to start the semester.

And yet, it was.

The lawn was suffering as homework, more so as the homework would eventually be finished that day. Patches spotted revealing a curved pattern. Each line bent as he strained to spy her bedroom window, which if he looked at the right spot at the right time, he could glimpse through tree and over shed.

The air was crisp with autumn leave and his mind was on her fireplace. The one whose smell always marked the beginning of the new season for him. The one that burned for years without him knowing who dwelled near its hearth.

Going back to retrace step and smooth patch was growing tiresome. Steam ran out like a deadbeat dad and smoke bellowed within. All he could think of was that fireplace. He stopped and stared at the hole between red, yellow, and orange and all he wanted was to be alone. His bedroom was the best place for that. Yard half done, the mower was left where it stood. October would come before the chore was finished for the final mow of the season.

The Zoo

The cotton head tamarins were shrieking something awful. Something had riled them up. Ms. Brennan's class trip making its way through provided an unwelcome din in the primate house and the sensory assault was more than certain simians could handle. With teacher's back turned, one rambunctious 10-year-old, David Nelson, a human, did his best to invoke the wrath of a razorback by pressing ham against the inch and a half of double paned laminated glass separating them. But the full moon stirred no emotion in the giant alpha male enjoying his afternoon snack of leaves and stems. Amidst the rustling of all these evolutionary branches, two clasped hands refused to break rank. Not in a showy way, they weren't the type. Rare was the occasion one of their impassioned kisses saw the light of day. A social courtesy as if disarray would follow as couple after couple would be forced to question whether they had ever actually been in love.

The passing shower that had chased them inside had begun its trek to the big blue and they were met with a cool humidity. He had purchased a green T-Rex snapper and, child that he was, kept using it to bite her ass. Then in true form would look up, wide-eyed and clearhanded, back and forth to buoyantly play it off. Always the sporting type she would follow suit by searching the area unassumingly for the culprit. Until she finally 'caught him' and gave chase. A procession of strollers prevented him from reaching maximum speed and he was easily caught. She took the toy and used it to bite his ears. A sizeable snack for such a small reptile.

Their very perceptible attachment to one another was the healthiest he had ever known. Several months had passed since he began telling her he loved her for sentimental reasons and would do so until days' end. Balance was achieved in keeping one another in check while extracting the best in the respective other. When he neglected to recycle his Coke can, she exhumed it from its trashy grave in lieu of the nearby recycling bin, staring him down every step of the way. When she began chewing her Big Red too loudly, his mock chewing shut her up quick. Even if she stared him down for that too. When he made a comment off color and surprisingly somewhat misogynistic, she smacked him in the mouth. Then upon his begging her pardon, she accepted with a kiss on the cheek. While standing in front of the rhinos, she began to freak out about college. He made her dance. At once her heart was light and her mind was at ease. The song on nearby speaker probably should have been *Young At Heart*, but *Swingin' On A Star* would certainly suffice.

The tigers were her favorite. She would never admit it. She claimed to love all animals equally. And for the most part she did. While some patrons saw them as lazy, she saw them as patient. While some handlers found them to be finicky, she knew they were just particular. And while some took their lofty prowling as arrogance; she was keen to their subtle intellect.

The Siberian Snow variety, they were among the farthest from home. But with two square meals a day and all the admirers they could handle, no complaints would be heard. She was their biggest fan and as a result they would spend the longest time in their presence. A slight attack of boredom hit him about halfway through. Though he dared not utter a word. Instead he wrapped her tighter in his arms and rested his face in her hair. Ocean Breeze? No. Rainforest something or another. Or Forest Rain. Whatever. All of her shampoos and products had those kinds of names. Tropical Escape. That's it. Whatever its name, it was hers. He would have gladly breathed it all day. But hunger struck and now she was on the clock to see the giraffes before they would grab a late lunch at the café downtown.

The reticulated giraffes carelessly swatted flies from their hind side with their tails. They turned a dull gaze towards the crowd forming and were not visibly impressed. She watched them doing nothing and even she grew bored. The way they clumsily chewed acacia leaves made her instantly aware of the rumble in her stomach and her desire to continue pointing out how cute everything was was overcome by the rumble in her stomach. To his relief, it was time to go.

A Small Café

Slight gusts were kicking up. Spring breeze had yet to turn to summer wind. The hair blowing into her face didn't seem to bother her nearly as much as it would have him. Rare were the instances where he would let go and get a buzz cut. Summer fast approaching, he had at least one more season cutting lawns. A handsome leonine mane may have made ladies swoon, or so he chose to believe, but it accelerated sweat production to unbearable proportions.

The table saddled the corner of the restaurant. Sitting on different streets made no dent in their afternoon. The metal chairs weren't the most comfortable, small price to pay to dine al fresco. Their habit of ordering too many appetizers had once again gotten the better of them and their entrees sat unfinished. Decisions weren't their strength. Which meant at that age they were right on point with their peers. After what was surely more deliberation than that which went into the Manhattan Project, they decided to go for everything they wanted.

Lunch needed to be complimented. Not that it wasn't transcendent. Hard shell beef tacos for him, spicy chicken quesadillas for her. Ceviche with shrimp, baby scallops, pico and fresh lime, wild boar empanadas, homemade tortilla chips, homemade guac to start. It was BYOB and she had by means unspoken provided them with a bottle of tequila. The staff provided the lime juice, triple sec, glasses and salt.

Unlike the atom, her attention could not be split. Flies passing by had to reroute because nothing could break her stare. All bugs pull up.

Then something crashed into her cheek. Nearby milkweeds must have lost contact with the control tower and a small white craft had to make an emergency landing. Before he could see what it was, it rest in the palm of her hand. Jaw dropped, she turned to look down her street.

"Can you see anything?" he asked in a voice he had only ever used for her, still puzzled, but ever accommodating. She nodded excitedly. He leaned forward, imploring her to elaborate just a little. "Things." He sat back. "Things?" he encouraged. "Yes, wonderful things."

True to form, she jumped up and disappeared around the wall. The seeds, known colloquially as 'wishies,' flurried a wonderland in the oldest district of the metropolis. He rounded the corner to find her spinning methodically. Evenly. As if she were locked into a track. Her arms outstretched, they tail-spun any milkweed seed in vicinity.

Their waiter, Carter, a nice young man under the impression that he was simply working his way through college and not going to get stuck in restaurants forever, had a minor heart attack when he saw the deserted table. He caught himself from bussing the table, and cursing, when he noticed her windbreaker still resting on the back of her chair.

Eyes closed, wishy landed dead center of her face, fingers spread, this star-nosed mole was in her glory. Happiness she never knew. With the man she loved. Not a soul on the planet with whom she would rather share this sanguine moment.

Though he couldn't be certain, and it seemed like pretty long odds, he could have sworn he heard Marion's Theme playing softly nearby. He was the first thing she saw when she finally opened her eyes. Adding the proverbial cake icing, she ran over to him and threw her arms around his neck and kissed him. What a handsome sight. What a sharp couple. Surrounded by wishes unmade.

Mam'selle

Labor Day Weekend to the workforce, it was another occasion for celebration to them. Either way it meant a trip to the beach.

It had been hours since they had shoes on. Sand between toes, in toenails, and just about every other imaginable crevice as they had been in and out of the water all day. She was turning red, despite relathering twice. He was golden brown and soaking it up, despite being Irish. Lucky bastard.

The waves were calm today turning boogie boards from amusement to furniture. Arms around her knees, she gently rearranged grains as he stood up for another dip. Without hardly any warning he took off sprinting toward the surf anxious to rid himself of sweat and heat exhaust. Leaping gallantly into the air, he landed with what had to be the least graceful dive she, or any other beachgoer that day, had ever seen. There must have been no sharks in the area as all that flailing would have secured him coming back in more than one piece.

When he was done horsing around he lumbered back to their spot chasing gull and crab into opposing directions. She was where he left her sitting on his board. Right where he wanted. He plopped down in the beach chair with a "Phew. Be a dear and pass me my towel." Following request, she picked up his Bugs Bunny beach towel, which he still sported with beaming boyish pride. As she lifted it, she heard a thud on the board. While he dried himself with an image of his childhood hero leaning nonchalantly against a mailbox and casually chewing a carrot with plenty of green leaves on the end over a hole in the ground, she inspected the source.

A dark blue velvet jewelry box that matched the ocean when the sky was overcast lay on the sandy, unused, light blue 40" boogie board that matched the sky when it wasn't. "Hmm, that's weird," he said as if she wasn't already making a face that screamed she knew it was for her. She hesitated. "Can I open it?" He shrugged. "I'm not stoppin' ya."

She could have fooled prying sun tanners through shaded glass to thinking Atlantis had been discovered. Two shiny starfish appeared. Pipers against shore and pelicans perched near dune blinked from the glare. Not real diamonds, but close. Rocks unearthed of the same design.

As she book ended her face, melancholy struck. "Oh no." Head tilted, he asked, "You don't like them?" "I love them, but your present is nothing this good."

"Did *you* get it for me?" he asked lobbing up an easy answer. "Not yet." He laughed. She always managed to surprise him with her answers. "But it will be from you?" She nodded. "Then I'll love it. Can I expect it soon?" he changed directions. She inhaled deep. "Yes." "Right now?" he pushed. Another inhale. "Yes." She stood and walked behind him, putting her hands over his eyes. "Close your eyes," she commanded. He obeyed without pointing out the obvious defeated purpose. "Now march." Step to, he also stood and began walking forward. The sand from their blanket to the boards was scorching, but he paid it no mind. No mind was paid to the threat of splinters once they reached the boards either. He knew where they were going. And he couldn't wait.

There was no line. Which was good because he couldn't see where he was going. She didn't have a lot of money. It had been insisted that she focus on her studies. Strongly insisted. An insistence that precluded her from taking a part time job. So a sundae at his favorite ice cream parlor was really all she could afford. So happens it was all he really wanted.

Three scoops of homemade peanut butter ice cream with chocolate swirls and broken peanut butter cups infused, dressed with "Reese's Piec-ees" (a misnomer he perpetuated), topped with chocolate syrup and whipped cream. On a bench at the edge of the boards in front of the shoppe, it would have precious little time to melt given the ferocity with which it was consumed. A double scoop of French vanilla on a waffle cone was her indulgence and naturally it prompted him to tease her with his guttural, over-the-top, cartoonish French stereotype impression, exclaiming "Sacre Bleu" and laughing "haw-haw" with every lick.

People watchers took hold. They were boisterous and playful and not embarrassed in the least when trails of ice cream landed on chest and breast. Elation halted only briefly when their future came up once more and she slipped and told him of the time she almost took her own life. For but a moment the treats weren't swallowed so easily. Sentiments exchanged and they soon returned to jesting and cheap stereotypes. 'Mon cheri' had done well. It was the best gift he had ever gotten.

Orbis Non Sufficit

He couldn't sit back. The couch was off white and she would be in big trouble if he did. He really needed to, but he was waiting for her to return with peas. She was also fixing him an iced tea and dampening a rag. It had been raining all day. He was such a boy. Whenever it did, he would always ride intentionally through puddles. The spray kicking off his back tire would rooster tail and speckle a line down his back.

She returned and rag was applied to shirt and tea was applied to throat and peas were applied to eyes. The shots the other kids got in made his shirt the least of his worries. But not the least of hers. If a reverse skunk stripe was left on the couch, she was a goner.

He had never been in love before. And as far as he knew, no one had ever been in love with him. It was unsettling in the best way possible. Emotions weren't really his strong point, at least not in a traditional sense. Never cried at funerals. Didn't think most people were funny. Never felt guilty if the other person deserved it. Never felt slighted if he didn't deserve it. Didn't even understand the concept of 'being happy for someone else.' Let them be happy for themselves, what the hell did they need him for. Babies, puppies, and piglets were never 'cute.' He wasn't a psychopath. At least not in a traditional, textbook sense. For him, to be this overwhelmed with an emotion, directed towards another human being no less, was a big deal. A very big deal.

An aimless afternoon bike ride. One street led to another and before he knew it, he was blocks away. One too many afternoons where the phone rang and she was in tears on the other end. No longer could he stand it. And she left to clean his mess.

What an idiot. What a... big dumb idiot. Her frequent warnings were futile combating teenage ego.

Those boys wouldn't bother her anymore. He joked that they walked away unscathed, but in actuality he didn't do half bad. There was some considerable damage done to the three and the fact that he'd gotten away with a few minor, quick to heal injuries and his trusty, hand-me-down Mongoose was something of a miracle. The bike was in better condition than he, but given he couldn't presently afford a new one, he was fine with that. She inspected the couch when his nose started bleeding again and he ran upstairs to the bathroom to rinse. Not too bad. As he stumbled his way back downstairs he almost stepped on poor Galileo who had scampered halfway up the stairs and meowed to ask if he was ok. When Gal took off back down, her parakeet with broken wing, Icarus, started chirping up a fuss. Icarus was one of many feathered Skittles to pass through her house. Birds had always taken a liking to her, they seemed drawn to her magnetism. He sipped, then placed his tea down. She moved it to a coaster he couldn't see as a Jolly Green Giant halved his vision.

In her best Ravenwood, she kissed each of his respective wounds. The damage was done and the 'I told you so' could wait. The back of his shirt was nearly mud free, but it still had to dry. He laughed under frozen veggie and she aped. "You're such an idiot." At the very least he kept things interesting. Back dry enough, he emptied his pockets and took off his watch. Scratched in a scuffle, it still told time. With empty pockets, swelling subsiding and back demudded and less damp, he sat back and relaxed. She rubbed his head as he turned to her and looked at her with one good eye to casually ask what was for dinner. Realizing she wasn't even the slightest bit mad, she exhaled and told him he could have whatever he wanted. Immediately succeeding a grossly inappropriate comment, he handed her the remote. Channel surfing commenced and pizza was ordered.

Glare

It wasn't his fault.

Had they been at the beach or in the mountains or back home or anywhere in between he might have made something out. Sure, given some time he would have eventually spotted a dragon, or at the very least, a centaur. But here, where city meets the sky, he just couldn't get a visual.

The movie was probably over or ending by now. Dwindling night owls were being reminded that it's not whether you win or lose; it's whether you get the girl. And speaking of which, Gillian what's-her-face still had a few more hours of restful slumber before he would craft a clumsy excuse and convince her to leave without being fed breakfast.

There was a stillness in the air now. In much the spirit of the band playing on for only two, crickets crossed legs in soothing familiarity.

He knew why she was there. Even before she had told him, he knew why she was there. They had possessed a sixth sense about one another since the day they met. When he opened the door and stepped outside, and she finally got to it, he had allowed her, for the first time in their relationship, to tell him her news without guessing it first. And, quid pro quo, seeing right through him and having picked up on his intentional ignorance, graciously accepted his courteous gesture. She rubbed her eyes to set back the contacts, which had drifted at glacier's pace over the tears. Her stance shifted and she looked up at him with the same expression as the night of that house party so many years ago.

"He proposed," she said reaffirming her big announcement. Confirmed was his theory that this was no ordinary visit and that her boyfriend had found a niche in her heart that he never could.

"And you said…" he asked in comical defense. In a falsely supporting gesture he kissed her forehead and contemplated how the man whom he had consistently viewed as inferior, both for her and to himself, had succeeded where he once failed. He assured her that she would be very happy and joked that she could do a lot worse, though he wasn't sure of either.

They talked on his front stoop for a considerably long time, even for them. As per usual, he hid behind sarcasm. She did her best to hide her remorse. She would later be overjoyed to tell her people and others, but as for the first person, he who specialized in making people feel bad in good situations and even worse in bad situations, it was particularly difficult. And it should be placed into minor consideration that a part of her still loved him. Finally came the part he used to hate. She had to go.

When they were together he always pushed for her to stay an extra hour or even half hour. Every minute counted and it would often lead to fights, but he never minded for as far as he was concerned he was battling for a noble cause.

This time he made no plea for her to stay longer. Another first. "Are you happy for me?" she asked as innocently as could be. "Of course I am," he lied.

On tip toes she hugged him, kissed him on the cheek, perhaps missing her true target, and held tight. She would never admit it was a moment she wished would last forever and had her arms not begun to hurt she may have never let go. He smiled weakly and assured her he would 'see her later,' still incapable it seemed of ever saying goodbye to anyone. It was truly goodbye, if ever there was one. She was leaving him behind for a life of Christmas cards, occasional phone calls, and chance meetings at public events. For cookouts and picket fences. Doing her best not to avoid another tidal contact shift, she walked home shivering in the coolness of late night. The kind of night that reminded her of long walks on the golden sands of the Eastern Shore with her best friend and first true love. Longing to come up with just cause, but unable to find any, he watched silently as she disappeared down the street where he lived. Turning his focus upward once more he looked hopelessly beyond the skyline at what was left of an ocean of stars. Instead the cosmos played hide and seek for someone whom for once was in no mood for games. Through tear filled eyes he gazed upon a lonely night sky and whispered in a voice he had only ever used for her. "I'll always love you," he said. "Just like I promised I'd do."

PART II

Special Delivery

She still got up early. The kids were grown now and the years where she had to be up early for them and the days where they still spoke to her regularly had long since passed. She still never slept. The pills saw to that. Luck presided only in that her curse never led her down darker paths to cheaper, stronger demons. Against all odds she tight-roped between favor among friends and loved ones and complete isolationism. Her map maintained the ruins of a few burned bridges and scars of scorched earth and until that morning she believed him to be one of them.

She watched as what she could only conject was a moving truck for one of her neighbors parked across the street. Three workers, very Union, unloaded themselves before turning to the cargo. Joe Kelly, 47, looked 67, lumbered over as she reached down for the morning paper. His suspenders had their work cut out for them, but the sun didn't. Barely up and he already couldn't keep the sweat from his eyes. Clinging to a dying tradition, he passed a clipboard, with actual paper, and pen to her. In order to free her second hand she placed her coffee cup with the crudely drawn sailboat down and signed. The other two teamsters had lifted the back hatch and had correctly guessed that she would, as they already had the enormous package halfway onto the ramp. Joe returned to their side to bark directions. The package itself looked entirely too immense for them until she moved to the street to get a better look, giving them a better view of her in her bathrobe and her a glimpse at the extra two movers still in the truck.

The five men very slowly and very carefully allowed the box to roll down the ramp, Joe snapping at her to back up so she didn't get hurt, or in the way, and snapping at them to take it easy. As if they wanted to do otherwise.

It was right about the center of the front yard when her boyfriend/fiancé finally emerged from the domicile to witness the shadow fall over his freshly mowed lawn. Blinking several times he strained his neck sideways and almost resisted the urge to ask. Though he'd only known her a few months, Mike knew better than to question the insanity that seemed to follow her around. But the delivery that eclipsed, leaving his hydrangeas in darkness was enough to drag him in. The paper she had signed came with a letter. Complete with a not so familiar return address, but very familiar name. Good thing her robe had pockets. "Hunny, what is all this?" What a silly question. The box wasn't open yet. "I don't know." She didn't. "Well, who sent it?" She assured him she had no earthly idea. "Hmm." He pondered. "Ok, well be careful and have fun. I'd stay, but I'm already late."

A quick kiss and a scuttle to his luxury sedan and she was free to unsheathe the letter. Her mouth was watering. Catching any run off, she bit her lower lip, her eyes gleaming. Lacking a letter opener, her finger slid confidently beneath the fold with nary a paper cut. As she removed the sheet from within there was a rather unceremonious dropping of just one of the box walls. She expected a reveal through full blossom, but with the other walls erect her only clue was a mysterious red glow suddenly cast on the side of the house. The five plodding brutes continued prying as she unfolded the letter.

Event Horizon

He'd been warned. The ride was providing more than enough distractions. Pagers buzzed ten minutes ago and they were on their way. Karl Schwartz, male, 24, factory worker. White, tall and thin, with a chin strap and a real sense for street fashion. He ruined his knees in high school playing baseball. The former Wildcat faced the mound for three years and one blowout too many later, found himself overprescribed to painkillers. A hop, skip and a jump over to heroin landed him unconscious in the back of this ambulance. There wasn't a whole lot these two EMT's could do. They had brought back from the brink. Maybe his heart wouldn't give out.

Sirens blaring, the ambulance bounced up and down as it blazed through red lights and stop signs. Schwartz lived in the back annals of the rough part of town, a far cry from the hospital. The driver was moving like a bat out of hell and maybe this guy had a fighting chance. Already a rough week, they weren't going to lose another. The roller coaster ride and imminent death did little to take his focus off of her ponytail. Even as he numbly checked Schwartz's vitals.

Her roots were starting to peek through. Swinging from side to side with every tremor, dangling gracefully from the back of her ball cap as she drove. He wasn't staring. Such close quarters would never allow a voyeur discretion. And he wasn't the type. Healthy curiosity, not obsession, kept his eyes darting. Something about it was causing arousal to well up within. They'd known each other for over a year. She worked night shift for the heightened pay so it was the rare treat they got to work together. His usual partner was in the process of leaving and he needed the extra money anyway, so it seemed as though it may become a regular thing. While waiting for calls their favorite pastimes included doing the Metro crossword, playing cards, and flirting, which ranged from casual to straight raunch. Harmless enough. Afterall, she was married. With children. But he rarely flirted without motive and his track record had grown to be something to admire. He knew how to talk and was quick with the draw. The golden loop wrapped around her delicate digitus medicinalis made him slow to fire. Most looking in would have said they were the last two likely to get together. Cliques, gossipers, and judgmental social circles could make no sense of it. They all laughed. Night in and night out, four weeks passed in that ambulance so close to his new partner. By the time they would get together, it was serendipity.

They had arrived. The doors popped open and as carefully as they could, pulled their cargo out to be passed off to actual doctors. Schwartz was in even more capable hands now. They were the best two EMTs at St. Mary's. It didn't matter. St. Mary's sported some of the best doctors in the region. Didn't matter. Before the dawn he would lose to the big H. Didn't matter. Sometimes they got follow ups. But usually unless the patient/victim died at the scene or in the ambulance, they wouldn't know what became of them. Educational guessing would have given them their answer with this one. She needed a smoke.

Standing against the wall, his foot on the ambulance tire, he placed his hands nonchalantly in his pockets, and breathed the sweet smell of menthols. Smoking really was never his thing. Every so often he'd bum one. He would try unsuccessfully to convince himself it was because he had grown a taste secondhand knowing full well it was to impress her. How sophomoric. But it worked. He looked surprisingly natural holding a smoke. Maybe not Marlboro Man cool, but it passed. Like any cowboy, he was trying to lasso something big.

With a final drag, he extinguished it with his foot. One would be enough. It would be years before he'd go from casual smoker to casual chain smoker. Not that he had the option, she told him it was her last then discarded the pack. Only issue he had, apart from the fact that he wasn't going to ask anyway, was that he noticed another pack resting snuggly in her purse. Naturally, he counted it towards her being conservative with her wares or to her forgetful tendencies. Besides, they hadn't even gone out yet. Her husband, loser that he was, foolish enough to get the hell out, was for the most part out of the way and she was fair game. In this land of beginning again all bets were on and grey skies could turn blue at any moment. She had no intention of wasting time residing in the past. He felt his back pockets and started looking all around. His lighter was gone. When he finally looked up and saw her standing with it between fingers, smiling devilishly, he knew it was on.

Jackson's glare was piercing. He entered the lobby to find Jackson, as well as several other familiar faces, staring expectantly. How the hell did they hear so fast. They must have been waiting to hear. It's not like it was a mystery. The way he and she looked at one another alone was more than enough to give them up. But old Jackson, St. Mary's most veteran janitor, had told him. If he'd told him once, boy. "She's playing you," he'd warn. He worried he was right, that her affection was nostrum to healing wounds, but it was clouded by the fact that Jackson was the type of guy who would call someone a liar to sound smart in the off chance he happened to be right. This broken clock made a face and looked at him through the tops of his eyes, snaggled teeth slightly exposed. Not a word was uttered, Jackson just shook his head. He had been warned. But it was too late. He was hooked.

Le Carnivale

She was staring at him. Uncomfortably so. He avoided as best he could, but it was hard to ignore and before long, he found himself staring at her too. They hadn't known each other long. He had to look down, she being a good deal shorter. They had already eaten, so he really couldn't suggest a snack. He considered turning on the television, but before he could bring himself to go for the remote, deemed the move cowardly. A connection was going to be forged if it killed him. Save for minimal, obvious shared connections, they did not have a great deal in common. Or perhaps they did and things weren't as strained as they seemed. His face fell into his hand, elbow securely anchored on the armrest. She mimed. While he found this throwback Marxist tribute charming, it had to be coincidental. Long odds she was a *Duck Soup* fan.

Show up and go was how most of his first dates began. This waiting period was really throwing his game. Then he noticed pad and pen and lightning struck. Pen in hand, he slid the paper over and drew a circle. Still staring, and she was so very lovely, so why wouldn't he, he clicked the pen, placed it back down on the pad and slid it forward. Stare finally broken, she clicked the pen and drew a smaller, touching circle, then pushed it back. He smiled. It was repeated several more times. Their common ground would come to cover an immense amount of property and it all started with a mouse.

Before they were done, the scrap pages would feature an impressive doodle menagerie that was destined for the fridge. Hell, maybe even the wall. The boys were roughhousing like lunatics in the other room. A bang was heard and received to zero response. A cry was heard, but still, nothing about it seemed atypical.

"I'm almost ready," a voice yelled from the upstairs. The two artists looked at each other. "Take your time," she giggled. It made him laugh too. Danielle K. McNamara was devilishly clever for a 5-year-old. Her eyebrows, definitely a product of her mother's genes added to her musings. Most of her look seemed to come from her mother. In fact, the only thing apparent of her father was her name. Her mother hadn't taken it for obvious reasons, but all the children bore it. It was actually somewhat of a miracle she had children with a mick. Given her upbringing.

With this deep and intimate knowledge of so many wonderful animals, he impressed her so. He had, afterall, been taught by the best. They flipped through the pages admiring their work. "Which one's your favorite?" he asked. As she studied the two-dimensional animals, her mother crossed the loft above the living room from the bathroom to her bedroom. As she kicked past toys not yet packed, she narrowly avoided cascading down the stairs on a discarded skateboard. The glimpse he caught revealed she had been spending the time on hair and makeup, not getting dressed. He caught his breath as her only daughter picked the drawing they made of a mother and baby elephant.

It reminded Danielle, Dani as he'd come to call her, of herself and her mom. It reminded him of *Dumbo* and he agreed it was their magnum opus.

The doorbell rang. The babysitter, responsible-enough 15-year-old, Kim Wu, from up the street had arrived. With her, a slew of games and one small, well trained terrier that they loved to chase around the house. And Kepler certainly loved playing the fugitive. The cat, resting comfortably atop the mantle and swinging its tail with no fear of renegade tinder, would remain completely unfazed by her canine guest. He crossed the floor carefully avoiding strewn shoes of mismatch and answered the door. Kim and Kepler entered ceremoniously and he assured Kim in not so many words that once their mother had more than a thong on, they'd be on their way and out of her hair.

Gets Up With Fleas

She lay on his chest. Her left shoulder tucked firmly under his right arm. Her hair frazzled and messy, resting gently over it. Her hand placed over the beat of his heart rustling around in his chest hair. Her breasts wrapped in a skin-toned bra and split evenly on either side of his rib cage allowed his pulse to keep time with hers. The night before, the dulcet songs of *High Society* echoed through the house, a favorite of theirs to watch together. Macaulay Connor and C.K. Dexter Haven both in ignoble pursuit of the affections of Miss Tracy Lord provided a lulling soundtrack, but would not be heard this evening. Tonight, it was a movie he deemed more appropriate for the holiday. It was tradition for him each year to indulge a few nice cocktails and watch the immortal 1931 classic, *Frankenstein*. She asked why he didn't pick a more holiday appropriate film, like *Casablanca* or *Eternal Sunshine Of The Spotless Mind*. He quipped that it was because he preferred a happy ending. The film ended with a toast and the TV was off.

The sweet smell of her hair imbibed him and effectively worked to offset his incredible discomfort. He loved cuddling and her petite feminine frame consumed no space at all. The couch barely provided the real estate suitable for one adult, let alone two. Landscape beyond the deck seen through the sliding glass door had turned picturesque. A big owl flew by briefly blocking the light that showed the room so empty. Before them constellations they had spent the previous night studying between long passionate kisses and puffs of Marlboro Menthol Lights still flickered. On that night the space found disruption from frosty breath above.

Now, the stars and all objects of celestial being had taken their leave. Resting light-years beyond this cover of nimbostratus that tucked them in for the night, was presently releasing a heavy snow on the Tri-state area. In all of Christendom nothing granted more peace and serenity than a crisp winter's night coated in fresh fallen snow. Ambient noise done away with, the two lovers took full advantage of the silent night, lighting candles, turning the television off, and talking about their dreams.

Some normal, he wanted to win this award or to own a vacation home. Some odd. She wanted to jet ski in the Grand Canyon or swim in a pool full of Jell-O. After, they wrapped themselves around a good book. In this case, a collection of works by New England native Edgar Allen Poe. His arms encompassed her holding the book above, they read a tale of the macabre involving a certain swarthy feline and a thirst for blood. Just then Tabby, her Domestic Shorthair, jumped up on the top of the sofa scaring them even tighter into each other's arms.

A nervous laugh later and they were fully engaged. It was messy, clunky, and awkward. Her figure was less than Greek. And he may not have been the man some girls thought of as handsome. Neither seemed to mind, the only real speed bump occurred when he rolled over and kicked the lit Balsam & Cedar on the end table and breaths held as it steadied. Upon their return to their respective positions he noticed something peculiar. As he put his arm around her shoulders she tensed up defensively. Chalking it up to the moment prior and with no actual resistance, he started up again. But as the candle burned down, he found that while on the surface she was fully engaging, something was off. It was unlike any of his other experiences. Twitches here and spasms there. Unexpected jolts. When he could ignore it no longer, he asked if she was alright. She assured him she was perfectly fine and implored him to continue. It all could have been written off as playful, if not for the troubling realization that by the end she was no longer in the room. Both finished, sang each other's praises, and readied for bed. Only one would sleep. He considered with each passing cloud as he supported her weight on hairy chest and burdened shoulder whether their sex life would improve. Or if at the very least, subsequent rounds would keep her in the same room. They would not. Dawn broke. She awoke thinking he had only just risen himself and left the room once more.

Alone

Snickers seemed like a solid choice. He pressed 3B and waited for the coil. Its slow turn always created tension in the gut of the impatient snack junky. Jackson and Nurse Diana Reddy were at it again. Dry leaves unswept, blown in through the automatic double doors, crunched under his feet as the bar leapt from its perch. A spill down the hall was currently going unmopped because a visitor walked by the stand wearing a shirt with the Millennium Falcon on it and Di announced unabashed that she had no idea what that meant. Once explained, she claimed she really didn't go for that kind of stuff and the janitor who spent countless hours of his life fantasizing about a galaxy far, far away was left with little recourse but to engage in a series of playfully heated comments that inevitably led to an argument as to whether alien life existed in the universe. Jackson, on the pro-life side of course, offered nothing in the way of scientific fact, referencing almost exclusively vague tales of UFO sightings in trailer parks. Dejecting redneck hearsay was her main defense as a woman plucked from the Bible Belt with free time so scarce and precious to her, slim was the chance she would ever spend an afternoon learning about fossilized bacteria on Mars or the giant methane lakes on Titan.

Gold of day was met with blue of night and he had time to kill. She didn't work that night, he had worked the mid shift. She told him she was coming to pick him up so they could go to a late dinner. At a restaurant she had never been to. She had. Because she was starving. She was. First she had to return something to Macy's she had bought for herself. She hadn't. Because it didn't fit. It didn't. And that maybe they could go dancing after dinner because she was a really good dancer. She was. And she hadn't danced in ages. She had. That she was free for the whole evening. She was. Because the kids were at their grandmother's. They weren't.

And so the argument down the hall continued until he happened by. Not wanting to get involved, but unable to resist an opportunity to show off, he let out his best Chewbacca impression upon hearing the subject matter. Nurse Reddy had no idea what to make of the outburst so foreign to her uncultured ears. Jackson was equally caught off guard, but impressed at the replication of his favorite Wookie's infamous gargle and gave into a fit a hysterics. "So what do you think," he beckoned, "there intelligent life out there?" He stared at Jackson. "Intelligent?" "Yeah man, whatchu think? There aliens out there or we alone?" "Are we alone?" he echoed. "Hmmm." He grunted and stared for a moment. He didn't even think to make the 'there's no intelligent life here' comment, a joke so tired it goes to bed after Wheel. He looked aside, breathed in and answered. "Archaeologists have in recent decades discovered tools. Made of rocks and sticks. They've only gone a layer of earth or two down. In Brazil. Thailand. Cote d'Ivoire. They have dated the tools going back 700, 800 years. And they are relatively certain if they dig further they will find some dating over 1,000 years. Analysis proved the tools were made by Capuchins. Macaques. Chimpanzees respectively. It seems there are several species of monkey that have not only entered the Stone Age, but have been in it for over a millennium. You ask me, dear friend, if we are alone in the universe."

With devilish smirk and eyebrows arched, he placed his hands on the desk and leaned towards his now captive audience. "We're not even alone on this planet." He took a bite of his candy bar and left to wait outside. Jackson, confused by the response, turned back to Nurse Reddy and dragged her back to the trailer park in Dixie.

Valley Of The Kings

He seemed uneasy. Not nervous per se. But something was certainly off. They were holding hands and staring at corpses. Surrounded by them, men and women who had been dead for centuries. She had jumped him in the car. A parking garage provides an appropriate concrete canopy to allow sufficient discretion for such inappropriate acts of public indecency. The skintight dress she was wearing reclaimed its shape in the elevator. They shared wicked grins that peeled across their faces like twin supersonic jets tearing through the sky at halftime. Fire in their eyes, the grins remained until they had checked their tickets and entered the museum.

His continuous need to readjust his pants once inside was enough to keep him preoccupied. It smelled of dust and decay as they passed pillars that once upheld temples and courts. The museum, like most of kind, ventilated in such a way so as to diminish the odor of history. But the olfactory was alive and buzzing with the taste of a thousand lifetimes and the sands of time would not be swept under the rug so easily. Buried beyond the hall was the unearthed tomb of both pharaoh and peasant.

She was very beautiful. Curls flowed through her recently blonded hair. Her icy blue eyes darted from plaque to plaque reading brief summations of epic tales. Slender fingers extended from weathered hands slid across inscriptions, dates and digs, as if they were written in Braille. She couldn't get enough. Soaking in facts of history and science was something she took great pleasure in. Never formally educated, she attacked a chance to learn with far more vivacity than any academic. He adored that about her. Whenever he'd make casual mention of something she was unfamiliar with, she was sure to stop him and politely request he explain it. And he was all too glad to do it. So used was he to blank stares whose wearers would pretend to know with forced 'oh yeah-s' and 'I think I remember that-s.'

They stepped carefully and breathed slowly. So as not to invoke some ancient curse by disrupting eternal slumber. The gods had found a new home in the form of a metropolitan museum in the western world and they'd be damned if a couple newlyweds were going to change that. These two weren't newlyweds of course, but neither God nor man could tell by glancing. He held her closer with each passing exhibit. Wrapped his arms around for an aerial video featuring noted desert landmarks. A helicopter with a camera underneath it blew gentle winds upon a monument to Ramesses II, the nineteenth dynasty of Egypt. Before giant foot stumps, dismembered feet of a forgotten empire remaining in desert sand, his steady breath blew gentle winds upon her neck, until resistance was futile and she turned to kiss him. If mummies had eyes they would have been rolling along with those of the docents, guards and patrons in the immediate surrounding area. It was neither drawn out nor salacious, but certainly enough to make them 'those people' in a room full of prudish nerds. In keeping with true form to 'those people,' their cares were as lost as the rest of the artifacts buried too deep to make an appearance.

Missing Socks And Making Faces

A state of disorientation festered as longing for her return mixed with straining for content. Fragments muffled though hardwall plaster and closed door. Turns of phrase slipped through void of context. Platitudes common to local vernacular. "It is what it is." The weightlessness of that phrase bore heavy on his waking consciousness and distracted from other, more valuable clues.

The questions of why her phone rang at 2:14 AM and who was calling at such an hour were eclipsed by the reason for her need to answer. What couldn't wait until tomorrow?

Her responses ceased. Within moments he caught himself not only sitting up, but leaning towards the door. Perhaps she was at the mercy of a bore ass monologuist. "Something she's used to," his internal voice was often that of a caustic self-deprecator. Perhaps she hung up and had fallen asleep. Or even fallen asleep mid-sentence. Something he knew her prone to do. Then he heard a door shut.

Sparks of static electricity crackled as he rubbed his bare toes against the bottom of the sheet. Ever the gentleman, he had taken his socks off earlier in the evening before climbing into bed. No reason they couldn't be civilized. He couldn't see the time; she was back. The clock blocker sawed wood while he lay mad at himself for dozing off. Madder still when he couldn't see the time and couldn't deduce how much of his slapdash stakeout he had missed.

For what it was worth, it made little difference to him. He was just glad she was back. He slid his arm under the space between neck and shoulder and kissed her head. Then he started making faces at her. Not in a malicious way. Just something that amused him when he couldn't sleep. His brief nap was more costly than whatever he missed from her nocturnal excursion. He was glad he had lest he been tempted to go to the window, crossing that finest of lines from intense eavesdropper to mild stalker. The silly stream of faces halted briefly as she slowly rotated tighter into his grip, then promptly resumed. The catnap ensured that he would be up for at least an hour or two and his thoughts wouldn't be enough to keep him preoccupied.

When he awoke the next morning his tongue was out and left nostril raised and he had to wonder if the old adage of one's face freezing held some merit as it was a minute or two before stiffness subsided. Stiffness withstanding, he really had to pee. Up and at 'em, he needed his socks for the trek down the hall. They weren't next to his side of the bed. Odd as that's exactly where he had dropped them. Under the bed? Not there either. He sifted through a pile of clothes at the end of the bed. All white socks, no black. Then something caught his eye. One of the dresser drawers was slightly ajar. He couldn't imagine for the life of him what reason there could have been, but he checked all the same. Sure enough, there they were. He pulled them out and made a face not so amusing. He looked over; she was dead to the world. He raised them in the air as if he was about to throw them at her. Rough way to wake up with footwear landing on your face. But he never launched. He just shook his head and made his way through a hallway box maze to the bathroom.

Beyond The Sea

On this night, he had insisted once again. Since the separation there was only one person other than mom whom Dani would allow to read to her. Not even her father, who had spent the three previous nights hitting the lights, closing the doors, and completely lacking the interest anyway.

So he sat on the side of her bed, pages in hand, while mom sat downstairs on the side of the couch, wine in hand. A baby monitor, that had widely surpassed its necessity, allowed her to listen in. She wasn't the only one. Soon in she heard footsteps overhead and smiled.

A funny thing would happen whenever he assumed reading duties. His deep voice reverberated through the old farmhouse, rallying down hall and stair. Creaks on floorboards gave away the boys emerging from their rooms and forgetting their age, as they would both stand in Dani's doorway to hear the story. In this case it was a children's book about, of all things, roadkill and she, or they rather, were hanging on his every word. Enthralled audience sat downstairs too, straining over fireplace crackle and radio rasp. Volume down, she shared the moment with her children. It was as if that old familiar spritely nymph had flown in through Dani's bedroom window, returning from the land past the second star, the one on the right, to captivate. The only thing missing was his pointy green hat.

"For the sun's last gift," he spoke for the woodland village's raccoon elder nearing the book's end, "on any given day, is to light the moon and be on its way."

Dani lay fast asleep and the boys processed back to their rooms as he descended the stairs. Oh, what a good life this must be. To be so admired by the little people. They truly did love him. Job well done. Legs curled up, she poured his as he approached the couch, fully aroused. She was leaning on the couch's arm as she turned with his drink. Another piece of wood tossed and he sat with his drink to kiss her in a way she hadn't been kissed in over a decade.

He breathed deep as he pulled away, utilizing container as ottoman, and after sipping his Merlot implored, "Mmm soo… we're *not* going to the beach?" She turned her head, frazzled. "I'm sorry." He fixed her hair, placing it gently behind her ear and brushed her cheek, smiling faintly.

They had been up early enough, too early in fact. She had already been up an hour or two when he got to the house around 7:00AM. The intent was there. Throughout the morning as one thing inevitably led to another, as was often the case with her. It became abundantly clear somewhere between prescription drugs at CVS and "Oh shit, I still haven't gotten milk for the week" that they weren't going. By the time they left the post office, the second time, all hope was lost. They had barely walked through the door when her husband called asking to drop the kids off early. Looking pleadingly to him, he asked that they at least still get ice cream. Which she translated to the Dairy Queen drive thru, missing the weight of 'at least' and completely missing the point in the first place. Soft serve vanilla dipped in cheap chocolate would have to suffice.

He forgave her as he always did; not that life interfering was a grievous offense. She took his hand and turned the AM station playing old music back up, as *La Mer* began to play. Wine glasses down, temporarily they slowly swayed in a circular motion. He would lift her arm and laugh like a loon every time, as she would never spin, pretending she had no idea what he was doing. "Tweest!" he would mockingly yell, which in turn would make her laugh. But she stuck to her guns and refused to rotate. Their laughter turned to kissing. Kissing to passionate kissing and before long, passionate necking. His turn as vampire came to a grinding halt when she jumped back suddenly and asked what he was doing. Stunned, he didn't even know how to answer. She stormed off as the echoes of a singer long dead and no longer listened to trailed closely behind. She said something else as she made her way to the bathroom to inspect the damage.

Man, his hearing was terrible. She couldn't have said what he first thought. 'No pantsing fags?' That couldn't be it, could it? Never a homophobe and even if he were, there were certainly none around. And even if there were, he hadn't touched their pants. Few moments past the one that was ruined, it finally dawned on him. Processed through and now he just had to figure out what the hell she meant by it. But yes, he knew precisely what she said. "No planting flags."

Borrowed Light

It was hot. Even for a summer night. The heat wave that crashed over the city days before raged into its fifth day and the AC in the ambulance provided only temporary relief for the young man who would sweat sitting still in 75° next to a fan. There was a Gatorade vending machine on the second floor. Three weeks prior he wouldn't have been able to race up those stairs fast enough. But her answers had become shorter and her gazes distant. With each stair he dragged his feet a bit more.

He was halfway down the hallway when he saw her at the desk. She was filling out paperwork. And chatting with the nurse running the desk. She saw him coming, smiled faintly, and lifted her eyebrows a tad before going back to her paperwork. He passed by her without a word.

The lump in his throat was back. Gatorade wouldn't wash it down. He wasn't unsure of whether something was going to happen. He'd seen the needle. Now he was just waiting for the shot. And right on cue, the doctor arrived. Dr. Varoujan Boyajian, born and educated near the Great Lakes, was a skilled endocrinologist and one of the top specialists in the area. Which was saying something given the area. He was working later than usual, a habit to which his wife and two preteens were accustomed. His hurry to leave was non-discernable, mostly due to the fact that his office was on the fourth floor.

Lemon-Lime was his favorite. None of the other flavors looked appealing. A little acting would keep the secret well. His finger hovered over purple while the county's foremost expert in anatomy pointed out his favorite parts of hers. With no need for a second opinion, she quickly forgot she had an audience. The sound of 16 ounces sealed in recyclable plastic falling through the coin-operated refrigerator startled him. So distracted by a flagrant display of peacocking down the hall, he didn't even remember pushing the button. Overcome by thirst seconds later and now wondering if he was becoming color blind, he picked up his Cool Blue and headed for the back stairwell. Turning around to use his back to trigger the crash bar, he twisted open the lid to his least favorite Gatorade. An odd sight made him frown and pause before shaking his head and descending the stairs. Dr. Boyajian was laughing and crawling around the floor, hands, knees, and all. The two nurses were laughing in amusement too as the good doctor looked and felt around the desk. Taking a swig, he went through the doors, shaking his head, not amused. The door slammed, causing the doctor to pause for a moment, then continue searching. It seemed he had misplaced his lighter.

Unearthed

The room was fuller. Only a few boxes remained, lamps back on end tables, movies back in the entertainment center. Oreos back in the cupboard. His eyes wouldn't give her the satisfaction. Cold and steely. Dry as a bone. But he was betrayed in voice through crack and tone. He looked back at her, belongings in hand, for what he thought would be the last time and in his last address strained to speak one simple command. It lay teetering on the edge of his lips, but never fell.

The old farmhouse was supposed to be up for sale. It wasn't. She was supposed to be moving. She wasn't. They stared at each other, she too refusing to make her simple command. The doorknob grasped, cold and steely, he turned it and exited without another word. He knew it was goodbye, but didn't say it until the door was closed again safely behind him. Two steps out and then it hit him. Wooded pathway got denser with each tear filled step until beams shining through, causing polka dots faded, and his shirt returned to a solid color. The friendly big owl hooed to see if he was ok, but he was too distraught to offer an answer as he felt for keys.

The light changed. He sat there. Idling. It was late. Almost 2:30. There was no one behind him. No one else on the road. For blocks, silence. His heart imploded under its own weight and he burst into tears. Gripping the wheel so firmly because he believed he'd float away if he didn't. He dropped his head upon it creating a brief honk. With nary a soul awake, no one heard it, nor could they hear his tremendous sobbing. Wiping his face consistently, he began uttering a phrase. Over and over again. Like he was rehearsing for a play and trying to get the emphasis just right. I. I. I. The intersection became quite a spectacle. Don't. Don't. Don't. Too bad no one was there to see it. Want. Want. Want. He was blocks away from his first love's. To. To. To. She was the last thing on his mind. Be. Be. Be. He had officially moved on. And it was the worst feeling in the world. Him. Him. Him. Returned. He swore he'd never let it happen again. It wasn't love. Apparently, much to his surprise, it didn't have to be. I don't want to be him. "I don't want to be him. Please, don't let me be him." The words played over and over like a broken record. Like a shitty kids' song trying to teach an obvious lesson. Like a corporate logo written everywhere to drive the point home and numb the employees whose spirits had yet to be broken. His was. He wanted her back. But not just for her. Maybe not for her at all. He had been beaten out fourfold. And on top of that, there was his own interest. Himself. Was this it? Would there be another opportunity? The odds had seemed so stretched that lightning would strike a second time. The odds of a third seemed astronomical. At least in the moment. Had anyone seen him in this moment, their empathy would have been overtaken only by their confusion. "I don't want to be him. Please don't let me be him." Of whom he was speaking? A father? A grandfather? Unlikely. Friend? Colleague? Coworker? Doubtful. Relative? Idol? Fictional character? Perhaps. The last time he was here, distraught over his Sweetheart, the phrase was "I did my best." It didn't matter that he did his best. With the mom it didn't matter who "him" was. It was the feeling, not the intersection. And there wasn't another car in sight.

Damnatio Memoriae

Michael S. Collins sat idly in a meeting of no real pertinence while his mind was soundly back at home. In his yard to be exact, where his new girlfriend/fiancé stood staring in wonderment at a most unexpected gift. There was never a dull moment for the new couple, but certainly through no fault of his own. Migrating from the Rocky Mountains, through Tornado Alley, up to the Delaware Valley, the gorgeous eyes that had swept him off his feet preyed heavily on his naivety and the poor Christian who was efficiently making his way up the corporate ladder knew no better. Back home a mystery was being solved.

After nearly an hour of carefully moving one giant crate, they finally had it where directed, dead center of the front yard. Passing cars had slowed their pace. Drivers leaned out windows to make heads or tails of the mysterious wooden box. Edge bars cracked out, a few jimmies saw the other sides collapse. They dragged the boards back to the refrigerated truck. Their job was done. The light on the grass made the head guy, Joe Kelly's shoes, show red.

"Sign here." Her bare feet shown red as he pointed to the line with the 'X.' Her smile stretched from ear to ear as she nodded and signed her name. Kelly stared at the delivery then took back his clipboard, grunting as he turned. With little emotion beyond confused annoyance and irritation from being in the sun for more than a few minutes, he told her to 'enjoy.' She put her hands on the metal rim. It was icy cool to the touch. Clear to the bottom, it was the most beautiful sight she ever beheld.

Once again she got less than expected and read the brief message as the container was left sitting in the grass. Thunderous rumbles had erupted when they dropped it, removing the wheels. She could see what looked like a giant monocle with stained glass through the tops of her eyes as she focused to read. Made misty by the name on the envelope, she pushed on.

"Dear Miss Lord,

Many years ago it became apparent that I would never be given the chance to make all your dreams come true. Figured I would settle for at least one. Hope cherry is ok. Don't stay in too long, you'll prune."

The opening reference was lost on her. She giggled with anticipation as she dropped her robe. More modest underwear on the body of a middle-aged mother of four kept any passing early risers from rising early. She hesitated, savoring the moment for about a microsecond before doing a cannonball that would have emptied a normal pool. Slithering rather seductively, she made her way back to the surface. Her arms resting on the side of the pool, she noticed a post scriptum on the reverse fold that she hadn't prior. She'd spend the whole morning doing laps until all viscosity was compromised. She would read it before tearing it up and burying it in the recycling for her boyfriend/ fiancé never to discover. The request, though simple, forever unheeded.

"P.S. Give my best to the children."

PART III

Business Meeting

She was New York. Wasn't born there. Made it even more so. The chip on her shoulder was that of shaved ice and her heart was a vast expanse. Her mind was overcrowded. Diverse was her heritage, primarily Jewish, but a cultural mix. To say she was beautiful would be a terrible understatement, though beauty is easily lost in a concrete jungle. Far easier to let strangers in than someone who could be close and personal and so she often did. Impossible for her to sit still. Ever moving. Ever changing. A long, unappreciated history with an eye for contemporary fashion and one hand on the pulse of traffic prone public and the other on a dirty martini. Extra olives. Pretention and condescension came naturally to her, but she was not without sensitivity and was caring when it counted. She enjoyed the finer things, but she was no J.A.P. Terror lived in her past and present. But it drove her to be better. To work hard and overcome. To win.

She had come, as so many do, from another city, another place, another time perhaps, to see what all the fuss was about. To be surrounded by the tired. The poor. The huddled masses yearning to breathe free. She found a walk up, small, but in an affluent neighborhood. A tiny drop in an oceanic bucket. Her life was packed away in boxes schlepped up several flights. The only sign of life was the tick tock of an antique.

She had been there once or twice before. Never this far north. Never this specific. Her trips there had been largely touristy and scantly definable. It was too long ago and she was too young to remember. The last time she was there twin brothers guarded the harbor between twin cities. Watchful pillars of peace and industry. The pillars no longer stood.

Work dragged her down to Jersey. Or so work thought. Luckier than most in that area, she'd never been to New Jersey. Never had a reason to go. She had passed through during her move. Seemed as boring a state as any. The most she had seen of it was through an oxymoron known as reality television. Hardly an acceptable source. Her boss decided his staff needed a team building exercise and thanks to someone putting the idea in his head, Mr. Vellutato came up with a great idea. What better place than The Beer Convention held annually at the Atlantic City Convention Center. Dropping her bags at the Sheraton Hotel across the street, she headed over with no intention of driving back to New York later that night. The guard checked her pass and purse and she proceeded through the double doors. The room was massive. For the second largest beer convention in the country, it should be. She passed slowly from vendor to vendor. Her boss was already sampling beers from what had to be one of the most attractive reps in house. Her industry was a man's world, why wouldn't the beer industry be as well. Some higher up had no doubtedly selected this young woman, Andrea, to attract clients. Andrea was tall, blonde and buxom, hiding a sharp brain below yellow strands and a good heart behind a substantial amount of cleavage. And boy, was the line growing.

She stopped by, said hello, but was barely noticed. Vellutato was gaze deep in the bosom of the beer industry. Rather than waste another second making her presence known to an employer who had picked her for the same reason, graced with the lucky coincidence that she was also very good at what she does, she pushed on. She was on a mission.

Riddle dragged him over to Jersey. Or so Riddle thought. It took no measurable level of arm-twisting. The words 'beach,' 'beer' and 'free passes' all seemed to mesh magnificently, like three morning birds' song. The drive had been fueled by high-octane energy drinks and overhauled with classic rock. A last minute back out had left the trio a duo and the two buddies soon forgot their fallen comrade. The ride grinded to a halt an hour or so before nightfall at a rundown motel that kept alive history of quaint inns now overshadowed by towering casinos. They weren't there for luxury, though they could have easily afforded it had they chosen. The weeds in the parking lot and draft in the lobby did little to dampen their mood.

Pushing through double doors, they entered an alcoholics' Graceland and much like the proverbial kids in a candy store, they didn't know what to do with themselves. Riddle, a close friend and frequent client, was an odd sort with stringy hair and a blank stare that would lead anyone to believe he had suffered the long term effects of some horrible paid science experiment gone wrong. But he discovered old, suggestible Riddle to be rather enjoyable company and was all too glad to pass the weekend with him drenched in suds.

Riddle's taste wasn't all that much more distinguished than his own, though he did seem to have a nose for hints and a taste bud for characters. Their excitement and Riddle's palate inevitably led to their separation, a trial that would provide just enough time for his mission. A half dozen 2 oz. pours later, he stopped dead in his tracks.

Babble faded into background as his vision deblurred. A significant change in skin tone withstanding, she looked just like her. It was uncanny. Whatever deep, unresolved psychological issues were at the root of his overwhelming attraction remained inconsequential. She saw him. He saw her. They both smiled anticipatorily. Their plan had worked perfectly.

A Prayer In Memphis

His love of history and her love of all things old brought them there. The fact that ducks ran the lobby certainly didn't keep him away either. He pulled up a seat at the bar in the center of the historic Peabody Hotel and ordered himself an Old Fashioned. No brainer. She was already seated two stools down. The bartender was the only other person to be found, sitting any closer would have wreaked of presumption. The trickle of the fountain the ducks called home worked well to intensify thirst. She was busy writing something, dressed in handsome business attire and so consumed in her work that she'd yet to touch her clean martini. They were out of olive juice.

Deciding for her that her break could use a break, he snatched the opportunity. New York's overdrive, meet Philadelphia's struggle to relax. "Do you like quotes?" he beckoned. With the bartender to his left and around the corner and he clearly speaking to his right, she knew she must be the target. "Not stupid ones," she responded most curtly. He laughed, taken rather off-guard. "Well this one's not. I'm not big on platitudes myself. Have you been to the Lorraine Motel yet?" He lifted his drink as she shook her head. "What's there?" she ventured politely. "It's where Dr. King was shot."

Her face took on humbled expression. Not quite embarrassed by her ignorance. By that point, it could fall into the category of obscure trivial knowledge.

The moment and her expression were briefly disrupted as two mallards casually waddled by. The importance of colors in mating told them the one with the green head was the male. He followed the female at a steady pace, quacking with each step. Not sure what she did, but he had reason to gripe and she was going to hear it all the way to the fountain. After green quacked by, he took no place above her for not knowing and nodded to her drink in a prompt to raise it as well, as he prepared to deliver the contextomy engraved outside the Lorraine's front door.

"I'd been there before, went again today after I saw W.C. Handy's house." A day of respects. "If you have the means while you're in town, you should go. Anyway, there's a plaque out front with an inscription from Genesis. It goes-" he cleared his throat abruptly as he wound up. He also leaned back a little too far, forgetting these stools bore no back. A drop from his seat would have surely compromised the solemnity of the commencement. "... And I'm probably paraphrasing a bit here, 'They saw him coming from a great distance. And they said one to another "Behold, here cometh the dreamer. Let us slay him. And we shall see what becomes of his dreams...""" Even the ducks muttered not a quack as a relatively heavy silence loomed. Then, as she gave a slight nod of approval, glasses clinked breaking silence. Turns out the quote wasn't stupid afterall. Matching pair. She had a history and he was old. They drank and before long were at work scheming their next rendezvous. It would have to be somewhere between their respective homes. And it would have to be soon. She wasn't going to be interested forever.

Inner Harbor

The bump jolted him awake. Big as it was, the Megabus was not impervious to infrastructural imperfections. He glanced down to see his book on space study and exploration had not fallen from his grasp, in spite of questionable wake. Substantial time had passed since their meeting, since the adventure that was so good she invited him back to her room at the Sheraton without reservation. Time since he'd forgotten himself and forgotten her, now allowing himself to engage she that was from New York. The Megabus charged through Delaware, whose greatest contribution to the contiguous forty-eight was allowing access to better places. At least it wasn't New Jersey. He hated New Jersey, the annoying high-pitched neighbor. He had been there many times. More times than he would like to count with more friends than he would like to remember. He always sucked it up. At the very least, he would leave drunk. At most, in love. He had left somewhere in between.

He also left his car at home. Traffic would be heavy closer to town, tribe was doing battle with congress. She was driving so there was no sense burying it in a parking lot graveyard when he could just leave it in his personal garage and get there and back for under twenty bucks. A town known for destroying pretty much anything it could get its hands on, he wasn't about to leave a newish beamer on the mean streets of Baltimore.

Headlights shined back at him. It was the middle of the day, but before he had drifted off he turned to a page with Alpha Centauri A and B, quiet neighbors to Earth's own and relative neighbors to each other. The book went away and the magazine came out. Celebrity trash and wardrobe malfunctions would get those eyes open. He unscrewed the cap on his Lipton Brisk and took a swig. Sleep had left a bad taste in his mouth. He put the cap back on even though he planned to continue drinking, a strange compulsive habit he developed in his youth. A youth that grew dimmer and more distant by the day in a continually expanding universe.

She hadn't left yet. The drive seemed daunting. Heading southwest on deasil track. Their plans were to meet for dinner. Not much of it, but there was still time. Parked as tight as one could fit it between a sedan and minivan that morning, her car now sat unaccompanied and ready for takeoff. The mirrors didn't need adjusting. The air in the car was a perfect 78° Fahrenheit. Seat belt on, coffee in holder, granola bar in glove compartment next to extra napkins in case she spilled. But she wasn't moving. She had lost momentum. A trip planned for two weeks and for a very special occasion. An occasion she didn't want to celebrate. And she knew he would be perfect to celebrate it with. She hated that. Why couldn't he leave her alone. Why couldn't he leave it alone. Why was he so... nice. He didn't even seem like the type.

She didn't mean to be contrarian. Everything she hated about herself, he liked. Leaving them with little in common. Their long phone conversations had cured his adronitis, but left her feeling vulnerable. Still, the moment passed.

She convinced herself once more that they were going to have a good time and started the car.

Dinner was divine. Typical Maryland fare - good to the last morsel. Several cocktails had ensured no Old Bay remained between their teeth and no sense remained in their heads. It was a whirlwind of colors and music and lights reflected on the waterfront. Good vibrations echoed at every turn to keep them dancing and the spirit she instilled in him kept his feet from the ground. They wouldn't touch down again 'til dawn. A perfect concoction for dancing among stringed lights.

One bar led to another until they had run out of corners to drink in. All that was left was to take her by the hand and walk her to the dock out on the pier so they could truly play among the sparkles in the wake. A considerable distance from the action now, the songs played were muffled and indistinguishable against the riotous cacophony. So he stepped in with two right feet and a few favorites of his own. Her ear provided the ideal soundstage and her heart the most captive audience. Brisk spring breeze blew beneath a blue moon waiting to be flown to. He sang every song he could think of, even those that, for him at least, didn't quite fit. Even a blossom falling in a small café sounded well when sang with the proper intent. Besides, she was half listening and whole drunk. Singing turned to kissing and back again. The pattern continued until their feet, his still hovering safely above the ground, were too worn to go on. He had just finished listing sentimental reasons when they turned to walk back to their temporary residence. Moonlight became her as they retraced their steps, far less gracefully than they'd made them. Their day ahead would be crammed beginning to end with nonstop sights and thrills, but at least for now they were cradled in the dwindling spirit of some enchanted eve. She stopped him at one point, not blocks from their destination to hug him. She held tight, burying her face into his dress shirt, tie shoved recklessly aside. Had he stopped a couple Dark and Stormy's short, he may have noticed the small wet spots on his shirt. But alas. The moment was credited to impulsive drunkenness and they were twirling each other once more not a moment later.

Before they could reach the front, she stopped. Gazing up at him with glistening eyes, she told him she loved him. And he was nearly fooled. But he knew Tito, Jim and Jack do more talking than anyone in any given bar on any given night and this was simply drunken words arbitrarily aligning. "Ok hunny," was all he offered in response and she forgot so quickly she didn't have time to be offended by lack of reciprocity. The doorman thought nothing of it, given the hour, when they both bowed to him on their way through sliding doors. He even tipped his hat to these fanciful sprites and sent them on their very, merry way. They would go to two wrong floors before coming back down to the lobby, asking for directions, receiving a much-needed push. Then with a friendly concierge lighting the correct elevator button, headed to bed.

Ma Nishtana

The gleam was right in his eyes. Her bedroom faced a courtyard akin to the one in *Rear Window*. He may not have witnessed a murder as he woke, but he sure looked like one. He cringed as he moved out of the sunbeam's beaten path. It was glaring off of a large glass patio door striking a bull's eye between his. A few blinks later and a deep breath or two and he remembered his place. Back in town on what had to be his dozenth trip up. Her hair had somehow managed to maintain its volume in spite of their nocturnal escapades and it was the first thing he noticed. Next was the long sleeve, V-neck, sequin mini dress, split down both sides and tossed carelessly over her repurposed antique side chair with Victorian parlor game upholstery, which made him the envy of every single guy in the clubs.

A wicked smirk tore across his right cheek. A light blue, silk sheet hugged the curve of her hip as she lay perfectly still facing the opposite way. White wine and vanilla imbibed him and put the kibitz on any chance of a hangover.

He felt too good to be hungover. Maybe it was she. Maybe he was still a little drunk. Lips recoiled beneath his teeth when she moved ever so slightly, enough to reveal the top of her butt. He breathed again, eyes closed. And lay a hand softly on her hip. With a touch like a paralytic, she would stir no more.

The antique clock ticked steadily upon the dresser near the door. Its sound only carried through the one bed, one bath in the dead of night and wake of morn. Otherwise it was stifled by a city on the go. The sound was as soft and even as a mother's voice. Apparently it was equally as commanding as he was soon back to sleep. An hour or two more he slept. He failed to note the time as the clock lulled. A thoughtless dream played out in vague detail and ended in completely wonderful absurdity. Why would he be driving a school bus while simultaneously part of a class trip? And why would he have to jump off mid trip to descend into the sewers to fight alongside the Teenage Mutant Ninja Turtles? Nuts to anyone who believed that dreams bore the weight of meaning. They were always just a bunch of crazy stuff that happened. No deeper meaning. No purpose. No psyche. All hogwash. And besides, if there were ever a time to play around in the recesses of his subconscious, it was now.

In spite of his best efforts, Jedi style telekinesis eluded him and he was left to the mercy of his extensive wingspan to retrieve the remote control. More restless than bored, he figured a morning talk show would keep him under-whelmed enough not to wake her. Shifting ever so slightly with his right arm trapped beneath her neck, his left stretched for dear life. Using friction created between button and finger, he managed to slide it close enough to grab. Now came the really tricky part. They had been watching late night syndicated sitcom lineups and the volume was still at 14. To succeed, he'd have to be able to turn the TV on, then mute it fast enough so no sound could escape. Dexterity was key as he placed the remote on the comforter hovering his index finger over the power button while simultaneously bending back his pinky finger to hover over the mute button. Quick clicking proved a riveting success and he was a little too proud of himself for it. His familiarity with local New York television was limited and he inevitably settled on *Good Morning*

America. Someone was onstage outside the studio, singing to a huge crowd. He didn't recognize her. And of course he couldn't hear her. Not being able to figure out who she was would drive him nuts. The new anchor mouthed her name when they cut back into the studio, but his lip reading skills failed him. He repeated the movement over and over but nothing was coming to him. T something. Tracy? Trish? Tr... he had nothing. Definitely didn't catch the last name. Now he was bored. Also a little frustrated. The TV went off. The coffee maker was triggered and the antique clock chimed. She'd be up in a minute anyway.

L'Chaim

Sails cast, they pulled out of port at dusk with a route charted in the form of a giant circle. His inhalation of sweet sea air was interrupted for but a moment as a nearby smoker puffed his last before callously tossing his cigarette butt to the fish. The motor puttered gently, pushing them further and further from the restaurant wake free. It only had to take them so far before the captain could kill it and let the ocean gusts do their job.

Their meal had been sublime. Coconut shrimp and seared scallops. Fruit relish. Vegetable medley. Key lime pie and coffee. The only thing that could top it off was a sunset cruise on the S.S. Pleiades, free with dinner. And here they were.

The inlet split in two as they passed. The cocktail bar near the center of the deck provided libations to toast a safe voyage. More apt drinks they could not have chosen, she clanked her Sex On The Beach against his Pain In De Ass and they cheersed to better days. Though to his current recollection no such thing existed.

In conjunction with the sea, she cast a mighty spell. Bewitched and beguiled, he absorbed her words like a sponge on the ocean floor. She was tall, flirty, and irresistible. Their eyes remained locked as they sunk round for round. Swell and swill made staying grounded a challenge, but he managed.

A seagull yelled to them, begging their pardon for the interruption before taking his leave and disappearing in the opposite direction. It seems the beckon of spilled boardwalk fries was too much for his little heart to ignore. Once gone, splash and old time music were all that could be heard. Block after city block, condo building after condo building passed as what possibilities the future could hold were discussed. No mention of children or wedding bells were made as they each offered the other vocational options to further careers. He longed desperately to suggest his indifference in the matter so long as she stood by his side, but something told him it would spoil the moment. Intimacy through apathy was the name of the game. And he was going head to head with the reigning champ.

Like it was tripped, night was falling fast. Those condo buildings lit up one by one, with the individual lights twinkling on in nonsequential order. They could only resist each other for so long. The atmosphere was too romantic and they were too attractive. Far from tranquil sea, it was getting choppy and they made a game out of going limp when the boat would ride the growing swells. Closer and closer they were drawn until it was awkward not to kiss. Maybe it wasn't awkward for them, but it certainly became so for anyone near them and before long they had the entire stern to themselves. It was Baltimore all over again. He didn't need to sing this time; there was a speaker right behind them playing everything they could want to hear. Didn't stop him. The accompaniment merely ensured his lips were free when needed. A strong dip into a large swell made for a close call and the recoil splashed them something fierce. Soaked hat to socks, not a step was missed and they danced, dripping and shivering, 'til they met port once more. By the time they walked back onto pavement they had almost completely dried off. He wanted ice cream. It was the only thing he wanted since he got there. Well. It was one of two things he wanted since he got there. He managed to convince her to go, though she feared the damaging effects it would have on her waistline. They walked toward a boardwalk whose stores were few and far between, boards warped and worn. An ice cream parlor sat blocks away nestled between a hot dog stand and a t-shirt store that went out of business two seasons prior and her attention span would hinder any progress in reaching it. A wide-brimmed beach hat caught her eye in one of the few remaining stores, which of course led to all other hats and footwear requiring inspection. Their buzz was wearing thin and soon the need to refuel outweighed the need to satisfy a sweet tooth. Onward they would go in the opposite direction towards the nearest bar and the ice cream parlor would have two fewer patrons in an already struggling business. Back to it, shooting cheap liquor joined PDAs as causes of extreme nausea and the two would close the place down closer than ever. Seems he'd get his sugar fix after all as they headed back to the hotel for the other thing for which he had come to town.

The Lost Weekend

Still no word. He was certain this time he hadn't mixed up the dates. They had plans. That was beyond question. What really bugged him was never cancellations. He knew well she was busy, scattered and distant. He was busy too. Common courtesy lost in that excuse, however, was another matter entirely. At least let him know.

Dragging her to the City Of Brotherly Love was always more difficult than it needed to be. A major city like any other. One of a kind art museum. World class dining. Celebrated orchestra. Sports fans who were... passionate for teams who on occasion figured out a way to win. And quid pro quo. If it meant something to him, by all rights it should mean something to her. But still no word.

Tired of waiting he turned off the television and put his shoes on. A weary world traveler visiting Beirut for the third time inspired him to venture out into the city of which he never tired. Enough TV for the day.

First on the agenda, walk along the Schuylkill. The park would be teeming with dogs dragging sticks, hipsters whizzing Frisbees, old folk feeding fowl. Plenty of people watching opportunity. He'd leave his big black Frisbee at home as he would have no one to throw it to and locked the door behind him.

A mile or two into the trail and he was bored. And hungry. And damnit, he forgot his wallet. So he returned to his house in Graduate Hospital to run upstairs to get it. His downstairs neighbor and tenant, Vicki Corcoran, a woman he had only made the mistake of sleeping with twice, passed him coming in. She smiled politely and moved past awkwardly. He took the stairs two at a time and reaching for his wallet saw a familiar blinking light. He had a message. Hope sprang eternal. Listening returned him to Earth, just an offer for a gig. Next on the agenda was a late lunch at Penn's Landing.

As he signed the check and declined the offer for a small to-go container for what was left of his burger, he took a last good look at the water. Bodies of fresh water were never as appealing to him as the salted, though he found it captivating nonetheless. Shopping in Rittenhouse was next and he figured he would swing home on the way. Better planning may not have seen them ping ponging back and forth across the city, but as there was no 'them.' There was a nice dark blue fedora in the Goors Bros. window and if he decided to buy it he didn't want to have to carry his ball cap around. Dropping his hat on the counter back home, there was that blinking.

Multiple messages. As he ran through them he was glad he neglected to hold his breath this time. Still no word yet.

The streetlights flashed on as he adjusted his new hat in the glow of lamp-post. The Continental, size 22 ¼, it fit beautifully. Tilting it slightly to the side, he shoved his hands in his pockets and jingled his keys as he pressed his brachium to the post. This hat was a tad more appropriate to his sport coat than the bright red Phillies hat for which he traded it. Contemplating reservation cancellation, he weighed heavily the humiliation of being stood up, one he had become more than accustomed to over the years, against how hungry he was. Hunger KO'd and he was on his way to the famous steakhouse that was once a bank. Though to be fair it was Center City. Every building used to be a bank. He considered shooting home beforehand. Finding no viable excuse, he decided to go right to dinner. Screw it.

So stuffed he could barely move and seriously buzzing from sharing an expensive bottle of New Zealand's finest Sauvignon Blanc with himself, the final item on the list was far less appetizing than it was an hour ago. Barhopping with the intent to find a place to fool around drunk in public carried a much different connotation when done solo.

Landing on the idea that hard drinking could be performed as easily and far more economically at home, there set his new destination. He gently placed his smoking plastic back in its leather sheath and headed outside in search of yellow chariot.

Keys crashed on kitchen counter with great melodrama, as did the thud of wallet. He tipped his new fedora back, revealing a cresting wave of gray hair. Debating between radio and television, he compromised and popped in *Fantasia*. One foot helped another as he pushed off his Cole Haans. Whiskey bottle grasped firmly, he made the mistake of sitting down in his chair before searching for the remote. Back up, across the room he spied the bulb. No flashing light. Not a single. God. Damn. Word.

When The Wine Is In...

Summer was over. Didn't really seem to matter. Not at world's end. At 24.55°N and 81.18°W Key West cooked in a tropical soup year round. Just shy of 1700 miles from the equator, the island chain's hook hid its most popular destination from most major hurricanes, but not from that Florida Sun. Gone now for several hours, the effects remained. He sat, still breathing heavy in a rattan chair with his feet on the open windowsill. This was a surreal place. He never sat so near the ocean without the unmistakable nightly lull of the surf. And he'd never been geographically closer to Cuba than the nearest Wal-Mart.

His scruff was turning beard. No longer short enough for scratching an itch on his arm, he simply pushed his fingers through his softened bristles. Time had taken their edge making his face pillow soft. Useless to one as averse to cuddling as she. But she was asleep and facing the other way and he was in the window with his throw pillow face. Alone with his thoughts.

The water was calm. Even for the Keys. Reflective glow bobbed here and there, but an overall stillness steadied through. His eyes moved from end to end gently tucking the landscape in with his gaze. An iguana, up either really late or really early, scattered out from his daytime hiding spot. Foot traffic caused him to ditch his efforts to cross the street by day. Now he was free to do as he please. Bad news for certain nocturnal insects if fruit was scarce.

The lizard stopped, still as the night air. Still as the palms that lined the boulevard. A sudden breeze rustled the trees, knocked the shutters, flapped the blinds, tickled his feet and swayed the iguana to bob his head. She didn't stir an inch.

He slapped his left foot with his right as a mosquito tried to get a snack. Between the heat and extreme cardio, his system couldn't spare a drop. The few cubes he put into his glass of water didn't stand a chance, sips became increasingly tepid. It felt good to be back at it. She was more beautiful than he remembered. Only their third outing this go run and they were on an island getaway. Granted, the island lacked all manner of glamor, but that fit him well and fit them better. It was hard to believe that in the modern world in this part of the globe there were still rooms that had no air conditioning, either unit or centralized, but dammit if they hadn't found one. The room was part of an old house owned by a friend of hers on Roosevelt Boulevard in the northeastern corner of the town. Elizabeth Moore had climbed the ranks in computer programming and in her partial retirement decided to save on travel by buying a rundown three bedroom in one of her favorite vacation destinations. It would be another month or so before she'd leave her cozy New York apartment for the winter and took no issue and bargained no charge for her fellow Manhattanite to get some quality R & R.

Their bounds may have been overstepped when they tore into Liz's personal wine stash, but it was nothing that couldn't be easily replaced, at least not for him. It was too late for a trip to the store and they were feeling particularly amorous. Chardonnay has done wonders in the art of deal sealing.

The empty glasses were on the dresser to his right. Lipstick lacking a sealing agent reminded him which glass was hers. He picked it up and studied it. His thumb ran smoothly over her lip print, firm enough to catch every contour, gentle enough not to smudge. He pondered. He pondered why she was an outsider to two, rather than one of three. A quick glance caught her shifting where she lay and he returned the glass to its mount. In a complete fog she raised her head and stared at him blinking repeatedly. As her thoughts settled and her dreams finished ending a question crossed her mind and once more he saw her true self.

"Do you like me?" she inquired aloud. After she asked she rubbed her eyes, he looked like a weird blur. Once her vision adjusted to the light and her mind adjusted to being back in this humid room on an island in southern Florida, she managed to make out the expression on his face. Pensive his expression, furrowed his brow. The question of the question hit him harder than the wine. He stared at her longer than he needed to. "Yes," he finally responded, "of course." She didn't smile at his answer; rather she pulled her lips back into her cheeks, satisfied on some level with the response. There were no follow up questions. On many nights, either over the phone or in person, he spoke to great lengths on behalf of his affinity.

The bugs outside played their soundtrack right below the screened window. He breathed hard, his lungs working overtime to compensate for the heavy lingering summer air. Their gaze remained fixed in the darkness. "Do you like me?" He almost didn't bring himself to ask. She swallowed. Not from anxiety over the question that had never really crossed her mind. Just because she was still waking up. "Yes," she affirmed in a small, sweet voice. The rasp soothed his soul and the answer was simple, but gratifying. Not another word was spoken before she returned to her slumber. And they both missed the point. She didn't need to ask. And he shouldn't have had to.

Proxima Centauri

Balled in the front. With a very definite cone-like formation, faded. With smaller linear dashes on either side. Not nearly as bright at the back as it was at the front. The one obscure rutilant light making its way through the blinds of the window and traveling gradually with the movement of the sun casting a streak across the motel room wall. It was so stuffy, like there was no oxygen. The humidity had sucked the air out of the room.

She fell on Alabama the night before. Got in late so she didn't do much beyond check-in. Not that there was a whole hell of a lot to do. Recent promotion gave more chance to travel, making clear how little the world had to offer. What a drag.

It was almost time to get up. She fiddled with the fun size candy the housemaids left on pillows instead of mints. Cute idea she thought. Hadn't had a lunch date in some time. Wasn't particularly excited about this one. She made the mistake of calling him from the Montgomery airport and blew her master plan. With cloak in carry-on and dagger checked, cover forfeit and once again he just "happened to be in the area." Suspicions still felt confirmed of something wrong with this guy as the odds that anyone she knew 'just happened' to be in Alabama had to be astronomical. The new guy, Rodney Stein, a fellow tribesman, was last on her mind however.

He was. And that damn streak. And the S.S. Pleiades. She should have let him get ice cream. A subsequent trip to New York and she took him for frozen yogurt. And she knew ultimately he didn't care. Still, she could be a real pain in the ass sometimes. She knew it. Didn't do it on purpose. When something is of no consequence to one's self, easy to forget it may be of great consequence to another. She opened the candy bar and snacked on chocolate, caramel and nougat while she pondered. The alarm went off and a quick shower and pant suit stood between her and an awkward rendezvous. Maybe she'd set up a rendezvous of her own. Give him a call. Wait, no. Well yes, she could certainly call him. And soon. But given her coordinates, she could do him one better. After her shower she would cancel her lunch. Rodney gave her the creeps anyway. She wasn't sure which landmark she would go with. Either would certainly suffice. Monuments to a powerful stand. A different time. She supposed she would just go with whichever one was closer. Jail in Birmingham or bridge in Selma, affecting and probably boring at the same time. Whichever she chose, she knew one thing for certain. She would take the bus to get there.

Shabbat Shalom

For once, he was traveling on business. A friend at a local university burned a favor and under pressure he found himself back in Chicago. There was never any desire to return beyond his first trip, through no fault of Chicago's own. The buildings were tall, the streets were paved. The river ran and the statues were shit on. It was a city like any other. But the long weekend he had spent there so many years ago left a note of melancholia around every corner. He steadied his eyes everywhere he went. If he kept looking ahead, he might not see the bar. The deli. The fancy Italian restaurant or the steakhouse owned by a former NFL champ. The hotel. The park. Not really remembering where anything was would surely lead to unpleasant surprises.

Dressed, he was back in bed. Or on it. He wasn't familiar with local Chicago television, but since he knew he would be doing a bit of walking, he figured he'd try to catch the weather. Strangely, there was only one option at this hour. A beautiful young meteorologist, Chelsea O'Neill, 25, blonde and slender, who had grown up in Aurora and moved to the big city with dreams of being on television to provide her people with up to the minute forecasts, had some good news for anyone out and about for the day. He turned the news off. It wasn't her of course, but he couldn't stomach one more day of the seven day. Odd thing to be unable to handle weather. Chicago wasn't the only city to have some everyday.

The dining hall adjacent to the lobby designated for the complimentary continental breakfast was packed with suits. He didn't think he had to be dressed for the occasion, but his wrinkled, half open button down swam awkwardly through a sea of ties. Not that he really cared. He wasn't much for first impressions or worrying about the opinions of a bunch of strangers he'd never see again. The coffee was fresh, had to be. Moving way too fast to get stale. He picked over his fruit and the blueberry muffin he thought he wanted went relatively untouched.

Showering was not on the agenda and neither was changing. There didn't seem to be a need. He was there to be heard, not smelled. He picked up his school bag, having never purchased a briefcase to replace it. Dropping his plate off in the appropriate dish drop area, he grabbed a Chicago Sun-Times in the lobby and strolled listlessly through the double sliding doors. With several hours to kill, he would take the opportunity to make his way to Navy Pier. No memories waiting for him there.

What a unique and wonderful place. Rides and amusements comparable to those found at a northeastern seaside resort hundreds of miles from the nearest ocean. Finding a bench in front of the Terminal Building was no issue and he sat with the Windy City's sole remaining rag, enjoying glances of a great view between articles. The view felt familiar, minus the salty aroma. The news was the same. Major upset in playoff baseball. Political scandal involving unsuspecting interns. Mother drowns her four children in a bathtub. Going to rain again. They should just print the damn things a day in advance, predict the future. Same old song and dance.

A speaker above his head played instrumental versions of top selections from the Great American Songbook. He barely noticed at first as he turned from page to page. Had he, it may have hit him sooner. But it wasn't until one of the less popular songs played. The moonlight on the lake. The promises they made. And all in an instant the things they did last summer were as clear to him as ever. She wasn't the one weighing heavy on his mind. It caught him off guard and he wasn't sure why. Afterall, it was her hometown and while they'd never travelled there together in all their romantic ventures, she spoke of it often in reference to many of her friends and most of her family. The story about the time she went to a Cubs v. Phillies game at Wrigley Field when she was eight and inhaled hot dogs so fast that she threw up all over the stands made him chuckle, but the fond reminiscence would more or less end there.

His free time was dwindling and now dancing on a pier he had never been on in his life was all he could think about. It was time to go. He passed several food stands, but if his appetite was compromised before, it certainly was nowhere to be found now.

The University was south, but the bus he needed was north and kept close to the waterfront heading towards Chestnut Street. Hearing the song had put his head through a loop and his guard was down. So when he saw her sitting at a table near a window in a café for a casual lunch, two or three double takes were required to ensure he wasn't just seeing things. Again, it was her hometown. But again, she was seldom there. A respectable suit, who looked like he belonged at the continental breakfast, sat across from her. Pigs in shit would have been put to shame by his ear to ear. And why not. A gorgeous, successful, older woman made him the envy of the staff. She looked content.

Befuddled by the odds, he didn't stare long. It was rude. Glare and gleam shot across his right eye, temporarily blinding him and jarring him from his stance in time to move on and go unnoticed by the diners. Once safely past the building, he stopped for a minute. Looking back at the café door as another couple passed through he harbored consideration of going in to say 'hello.' The passion it takes to pump bad blood through one's veins had dissipated years prior. The only thought on his mind as he decided against it in favor of catching his bus was what had brought her home. As it happens, she was in town for a wedding.

The class sat with ill-developed anticipation. The only real bonus here was that they didn't have to take notes as nothing that would follow would find its way to test or quiz. A few eager students were anxious to hear what he had to say. That is until they saw him. He was older than they realized and more tired looking than someone should be in the early afternoon. He was slovenly, unkempt. Not gross or even ugly, per se. Just looked like had he put any effort into his appearance whatsoever, a different impression would be given. A razor and ironing board go a long way for a generation used to things being sleek, shiny and polished. And this dinosaur was about to lecture them for the next hour.

His speech was impressive. Clearly he knew his stuff. The delivery could have used some work. While his intellectual points were all landing gracefully, any attempts at humor either fell flat or were simply skipped. Self-editing on the spot became the name of the game as joke after joke was omitted. Not that it was a comedy routine, but the material felt dry in preparation, needing a spritz of humor.

The speech concluded with generous applause. He nodded appreciatively and gathered his papers holding his breath. Dread overtook as he hoped in vain that the inevitable wouldn't happen. Then, Professor Horton White, his longtime friend and colleague polled the class asking in the remaining minutes before dismissal if anyone had any questions for their special guest. Their special guest, gracious, yet begrudged, put his bag down and scanned the room. Northbrook native, 22-year-old Tori Beckman was the first and one of only a few to raise her hand. She was called on with a silent nod. "You spoke earlier of how availability heuristic is the biggest influence in all forms of writing, including the editing process. Could you give an example of a time where your personal experience really came into play with a project?"

"Obviously it'll have to be a recent example," he replied. Laughter was reserved to the select able to catch a heuristic joke. "I feel like a magician revealing his tricks." After a moment weighing his options, he noticed the same girl who asked the question, Tori, was wearing flip-flops with jeans. An odd fashion to be sure. He stared at her wiggling, open toes. The silence was growing. "There's a tendency to stray from logic when someone's trying to win an argument where they know they're wrong. Several ways it could be done. One great way is to take a small offense of the other person and make it seem much worse than it is. Act like a tiny insult is a grievous offense. All of a sudden 'why would you do that' becomes 'how could you.' 'That's not fair' becomes 'are you kidding me.' I was fixing a shortie pro bono for a friend and he couldn't get past a fight. Both characters were battling back and forth. Logically. He couldn't get anywhere because it made too much sense. Let the wild accusations fly. Men deflect and women project. And God help you if you logically box them into a corner. Forcing tears, why do you want to hurt me. Like you woke up this morning to go hurt her. Like it's your life mission." He stopped to breathe. It did little to slow him down. "So you have to turn the whole thing on itself. Think like someone who doesn't know what they're talking about, creating a literary anomaly as you're supposed to only 'write what you know.' Say whatever comes to mind. Don't be afraid to throw dirt in the eyes. Once you knock your main down, the audience will follow." In the heat of his little speech he had removed his reading glasses amidst talking with his hands. He replaced them to the bridge of his nose. Schoolbag on shoulder, he nodded to his dear old friend and walked out the door in need of a cigarette.

Tori was sorry she asked. He was sorry he quit.

Better Days

She had always wanted one. She sat, legs crossed, in her brand new bay window in the breakfast nook of her very old house. After pinching a few pennies over the course of several years, she put a down payment on a classic Victorian three story home upstate with a yard she didn't need and a garden she didn't tend to. The window was open a crack on either side letting in a soft spring breeze. It had been seven weeks since she'd first walked through the threshold of her abode as a homeowner. And seven years since she had said goodbye to the bright lights of Manhattan.

Flipping casually through a fashion magazine, she rested her head against the windowpane. A squirrel hopped along the wooden fence separating her yard from her neighbors'. A cloud rolled by briefly casting a shadow, sending a momentary chill that caused a slight shiver. The wind blew causing the old house to shift, the upstairs floorboards to creak and leaves that were very green to flutter. Logic told her it was just the structural insecurity of a building that had somehow survived into modernity. Superstition sent a second chill down her spine and she was now more convinced than ever that her new old attic was haunted by a colonial family that had died of this epidemic or that a few centuries prior. Such legends were played to death throughout that and many other communities like it, mostly for the sake of passing tourist. She had taken it to heart, however, and as a result the final floor of her home was off limits from magic hour until dawn. Typically, it wasn't an issue. But given she had just moved and half of her life was still in boxes, occasions did arise where she needed a colander for pasta or tennis shoes for tennis on days where she convinced herself she was going to actually play and she could really use someone brave enough to go up there.

Another page turned when a knock at the door caused her to lift her head. Brow furrowed, she wondered who it could possibly be. She unfolded her legs and hopped off of the window, a physical feat that quickly reminded her of her age. Her floral sundress rippled as she gracefully made her barefoot way across the living room floor. Reds, oranges, yellows, blues and whites flitted as the woman who would rather be left alone than loved set eyes on a brown hat peeking through the front door's window.

She opened the door most casually and without regard knowing full well a stranger stood on the other side and knowing full well the crime rate of her new township was practically nonexistent. The open door revealed his shirt matched his hat and his shorts matched his shirt. He inquired how her day was as he passed the electronic signature capture forward. As she looked down to craft a sloppy, squiggly moniker her eyes fell upon a small rectangular package. Her eyebrows were getting a workout today. "Your boyfriend must have jumped through some hoops. With the new liquor laws."

'Dave' was the name on his nametag. She read it as her gaze rose to his dumb face. Now she was deciding if she was more pissed at 'Dave' for his presumption of donor or his spoil of surprise. Not that a box of that height and width could have been much of anything else really. It was more the principle. She said nothing, giving him a nod and sparing him correction, and on his way he went.

The porch boards were cool to her feet as she stepped down to inspect the package. She searched for a return address finding one from California. In the Napa Valley to be exact. She didn't know anyone in Napa; it was likely the address of the winery itself. Dead end.

The package sat on the floor. The bottle on the table. She sat in her antique chair, window adjacent, racking her brain. It wasn't Greg. It wasn't James. Chris? Maybe it was Chris. No. No, last she heard he was happily married and expecting. Who could it have been? Pondering the mystery was soon overcome by a desire to host her own personal Sunday brunch starring her favorite wine. The quandary dissipated and the glass raised. *To... better days.*

364 lesser days passed. She arrived home carrying a bag of groceries and she ascended the porch stairs to find a canary yellow note stuck to the door. Her

old station wagon clicked as it always did after killing the engine and served as a slight distraction while she read the note informing her she had missed a package delivery.

Note in hand, she debated just getting back in the car. But perishables perish. Butter melts no matter how low the sodium, ice cream no matter how non-fat. And a fish that was so easily duped into a net days prior stood no chance against the greenhouse effect within the trunk of a station wagon. She unloaded her groceries with increasing haste as her curiosity compounded. Not that it was an unusual day for her to receive a gift. But what could it be. So wrapped in the question she rushed out after unloading her plunder sans her spring jacket. The hand-me-down tweed lay carelessly on the couch as the door slammed and she drove away.

The trip to the local post office was brief, not surprisingly. The wait at the local post office was brief, very surprisingly. She traded her John Hancock once more for a familiar looking package. Déjà vu all over again. She nodded to the teller and took the small, rectangular box with her. She was sufficiently weirded out now, the return address being the same as last year, but was eased by the fact that this particular brand of Chardonnay pairs exceptionally well with blackened Mahi.

The year prior she had asked around, thanked a few wrong people, even almost sent a Thank You note before finding out the intended recipient wasn't the culprit. The gifter never presented themselves and now she sat in her driveway, the engine clicking, next to the deaf mute. She held the steering wheel with its worn, sunburn leather covering and moved her feet slowly back and forth on a floor mat that she could almost see through. Fortunately she had outgrown shiny new cars years ago and had come to the realization that holding your breath while turning the key was better than paying a landlord's mortgage.

Dinner was quiet. She was alone, so there was that. But she had also neglected to put music on. No Glenn Miller or Tommy Dorsey. No Miles Davis or Oscar

Peterson. Just her and the bottle. All of a sudden she surprised herself. It was no longer troubling or weird. She was sad. Without the knowledge of the gifter's identity, she lacked the capability of giving thanks.

Years passed and the pattern continued. Every year on that day she knew to buy fish or poultry because every year on that day she received a bottle of Cakebread Cellars Chardonnay. Even after they stopped making it. Whoever it was, they were well stocked.

Fifteen bottles later she was sitting in the bay window once more, enjoying a glass and a half and it finally hit her. An article discussing Thomas Jefferson's affair with Sally Hemmings and John Adams' knowledge of it made casual mention of Independence Hall. This combination of elements left her mind with one place to go.

She wasn't sure why she had never considered him before. Sure, she had ex-boyfriends and ex-lovers with greater means. Even with his accrued wealth over the past couple decades, he wasn't even close to her richest former. But she was convinced now it was him. Yes, surely it was him. For he was kind. And he looked out for his own. Consistently misunderstood and grossly underrated. Could hit, but more importantly could get hit and keep moving forward. He was cocky, only sometimes with valid reason. He was older and dirty. But he was Brotherly to the right people. Well planned, ill executed. News oriented, but improperly educated. He was damaged, slow to change and hateful towards it. He was cultured, but close-minded. Reserved to stand in his own way. Undyingly patriotic. Stuck in the past. The eternal underdog. He was Philly.

And she was New York.

PART IV

Dinner

He came home from the market later than desired. Half a day at the office did not afford the amount of time he needed to combat the holiday crowds at the Terminal. Time was of the essence, she would be there any minute. And there was the strict curfew to consider. When days were at their shortest, they had the least time together. It wasn't that she'd be an ogre about a later supper, hard on him for his perpetual tardiness. A friend recently told him that he'd be late for his own wedding, a bold yet accurate prophecy if the day ever came. Another friend upon hearing this statement modified and told him he would be late for his own funeral. The laugh was short-lived seeing as if anybody could be-. Giddy anticipation teamed up with frigid air and was driving her from work all the faster. No man ever cooked for her before. He worshiped her. Worshiped the ground beneath her. She couldn't believe her luck. Which was an interesting coincidence because funny enough, neither could he.

He unpacked his bags with the same tactful precision with which they were loaded. He began with the protein. Two one-pound tuna steaks, ½ pound of jumbo shrimp, ½ pound baby sea scallops. Then white rice, wheat bread, butter. Next he turned to the produce bag. Fresh garlic cloves, lemon, lime, coconut water, one large white onion, a pineapple, a mango. From the state store bag he removed a bottle of decent, moderately priced, domestic, non-vintage white wine. He was only going to use it for cooking, but as a wise chef imparted to him, you wouldn't drink a cheap wine, why cook with one. Plus, it would make chugging it while cooking much easier. Not a drop to be wasted. He also removed a bottle of Patron Silver, she was a tequila girl. He removed a bottle of Captain's Private Stock, he was a rum guy. Thanks to her. And he removed a large bottle of champagne. Which was also decent, moderately priced, domestic, non-vintage. A little of everything for a special night.

He grasped the measuring spoons frowning. Even if he had a list of proper measurements in front of him, he had no use for them. Such extraneous measures weren't needed to prepare a meal when the cook bore keen eye and sensible palate. Back in the drawer they went. He had everything he needed. Placing the cutting board on the counter, he began chopping pineapple and mango. The onion was up first cooking wise, but it made more sense to cut fruit first. Sweetness in the onion made more sense that pungent astringency in these tropical delights. The chopped fruit was placed aside, board washed, and garlic mincing commenced. The onions were next. Tears were inevitable. Though it didn't stop him from fighting them with all his might. Three cups water for one and one half cups rice. Getting clever, he substituted two cups tap for two cups coconut. Once the rice was done, he added the chopped fruit and moved it to keep warm on the back burner.

Sauté pan began to sizzle as the minced garlic and onion petals were dropped in heated vegetable oil. Wooden spoon passed them casually from side to side ensuring they would brown, but not burn. Then in went the shrimp, which he deveined and peeled while onions and garlic caramelized. He tossed back a swig of the white wine and poured two swigs worth in the pan, keeping the wooden spoon busy. After he was certain the backside of each shrimp was pink, he flipped them to even the sides. The smell of his garlic shrimp was wafting, aromatic, but not mood inspiring. Candles set throughout the house of passion fruit, key lime, and cinnamon were lit while he waited for the other side to pink. Unseasonal for some, but it created the proper atmosphere for the menu.

The tuna, done right, wouldn't take long at all. Which was good because she would be over any minute and he still had to prepare the cocktails. He cut off a large slab of butter, about an inch and a half thick and melted it down in a large frying pan that usually only saw the likes of all beef hot dogs or grilled cheese. Flash frying would create the desired crisp on the outside, leaving the fleshy center tender, red, rare.

Four pieces of wheat bread were popped into the toaster. Set to dark. Once toasted and cut in half, they'd make a fine bed for the garlic shrimp. Ah crap. Half toasted and it hit him. He forgot the scallops. They might turn out a tad underdone, wouldn't be the worst thing. Same as the tuna, nice brown crispy exterior was key. Which reminded him. He sliced one of the limes and squeezed it over the fish and scallops. Another minute or two and plating could commence. Lime squeezed over the rice would give one last tropical flare to his trademark side. It was sticking to the edges of the pot; he had left it warming too long. A metal spoon scraped it loose and it was good to go.

As he was finishing the final touches, his heart jumped. He heard the all too familiar door slam as she came in. Quick like a bunny he dumped handfuls of ice cubes into two rocks glasses and worked up her cocktail first. Silver and lime juice, touch of Grand Marnier, and her margarita was ready to party. His rum and ginger was an easy fix too as he heard an unfamiliar rubbery sticking, sucking and smacking with each step. No further thought to it was given as she climbed wooden stairs and he patiently waited to see his Pretty Girl's beautiful face when she turned the corner.

La Vie En Rose

His time served in corporate America was short lived. Just shy of a decade. 9 years and 4 months may only be substantial to someone who never confined themselves to the living death that is the persistent sound of typing and bullshitting set to no radio soundtrack in the unholy and unnatural glow of fluorescent light.

Desk jockeys racing to nowhere on the wild ride of elevator stops with the semi sweet taste of kissed ass lost the sincere displeasure of his company several years back. Tooth, nail, and anything else he could swing or throw were used in his fight against normalization. Skipping corporate sponsored outings, using corporate charge at strip clubs, telling the government it was expense by way of business, holiday functions, picnics, happy hours. One hour of happy wouldn't cover the other eight. If he had known what it would have cost him in the following years, he may have drank up.

Her name meant something. The family had been an institution in the city since century turned and only an elite few were allowed in. Enough to eliminate the need for inbreeding. Noblesse oblige was duty, sentence really and while he was no pauper, when he left a comfortable position at a Fortune 50 to finally turn part time passion into full time mission, he sealed his fate. Afterall, her family could think of nothing more degrading and deplorable than dating a writer.

She was always the black sheep, pardon the expression, especially with the whole weathergirl nonsense. But while he would do what was best for himself, she was willing to sacrifice for legacy.

Quitting was done without tact. He colorfully illustrated where things could be shoved or stuck. His stellar creativity exercised to the fullest extent. While the unnecessary theatrics did rouse claps made anonymously behind cubicle walls, it was approval from those whom he needed none.

As he sat at his antique mahogany desk exchanging stare between photograph of her and the abyss, he contemplated whether the level of begging required to get his job back was surmountable. Freedom secured from corporate America meant freedom retained. Even if begging would work and even if the rumor his former boss had himself been fired, it mattered not. It wasn't the reason they broke up. Switching from desk to bed, he lay with hands behind his head a la Ferris Bueller. He looked at her side half expecting to see her, half asleep, ready for one of his trademark sneak attacks. Only the ghost of her remained.

The ghost in her was keeping her awake. She too had just given up on what she was trying to do and gone to bed. Futile, she never slept. Looking for him in his spot, but finding another man in his place. He was asleep and she thought about calling. But couldn't risk the fight if he woke. Engaged to a fiancé she had no intention of marrying, she knew her place. The light sleeper was a hard hitter. Marne Fleming knew exactly how to hit her where it hurts. In spite of great beauty and matching success, she was sensitive and carried the burden of low esteem. The man who knew too much in ways of taking advantage of the cursed groggily rolled over to make room for her. The man who refused to do so had plenty of room, finding only a long strand of iron-gray hair to play with. Convenient as gentle rest hopped in the backseat to let toss and turn take the wheel as he longed for the sleep that outlasts love.

Dark Matter

They never wanted the connection anyway. Had no choice but to deal with her, as is often the case with relatives. Good riddance. With the ties that bound cut, there was no sign of her or her kind. He was there. He never wanted these connections. As is often the case with relatives. The theory of relatives says that the innate drive toward survival keeps that which would otherwise be loner part of a clan. But crimson platelet water flowing through vein takes longer to dry up than love and when they saw he without his shadow and another by his side, no one bothered to question it.

For once he was relieved they didn't care how she was doing. If he had to explain why they were no longer together, why they were destined to part, why their all too brief love affair burned out before either was ready, he would be plagued with "I told you so-s" and "I knew she was trouble-s." Rather than the socially contracted obligatory "I'm so sorry, are you ok-s?."

As far as they were concerned, he was great. Their holiday party would go unadulterated. How dare a nigger, so sweet and unassuming, have the audacity to walk invitedly into their home anticipating common courtesy. Not even close to the reason of their demise, they went in expecting a certain level of resistance. On both sides. They were met verily. Truth was her prior history provided a lack in range of interactions needed to form healthy structured relationships. That wasn't the biggest reason either, but it certainly bore more weight than race.

But it wasn't Hatfields and McCoys. Capulets or Montegues. Respective universes maybe never collided; they were simply closer than comfort allowed. A few outstanding members of an endangered species taking final stands in the name of an ideology that, like rowdy cousin Haley after beer #14, had overstayed its welcome.

Complete cloud cover did nothing to reduce the unseasonable warmth. No threat of snow. Which was bad for the spirited, but good for him, he wasn't in the mood. The room was kept light by old comedy clips playing on television. Steve Martin dancing around served distraction for the deep impact felt at the recent passing of their dear great Uncle John. Motions and polite conversation got him steps closer to leaving. His guest was faring well, not that he cared. While Jan Lindsay spoke pleasantly with one of his cousins, Noelle, or maybe it was a second cousin, he could never keep track, he chewed carrot sticks and waited impatiently for an acceptable time to excuse themselves. While reaching for the dip, his Aunt Carol seized her chance to corner. After the ceremonial 'how have you been, how's work' she turned to something unexpected. "I didn't realize you were seeing someone else." His chewing stopped. "What happened with-" Like an old Chevy, her sincerity backfired when she realized she couldn't remember the name of the Pretty Girl he oft brought round. "Gone cold." He was blunt. More so than he meant to be, but his emotion was mixture of surprise of subject and desire to talk about anything but. Appropriate though, as they were always hot or cold. Jan was warm. Should be, she had four layers on.

"Oh, well," looking across the room at her son, Nick who replaced Noelle and was enjoying Jan's company a little too much, "she seems nice."

Chewing resumed. "Her?" He swallowed and took another bite. "She's a comet." Carol was heartily confused and thought she misheard. "I'm sorry?" "Don't be," he continued knowing exactly what she meant. "Iron of the sky. Like Tut's dagger. They come in hot as blazes and fast as lightning. Sometimes out of nowhere. Usually out of nowhere. Beautiful to look at, dangerous to touch, and impossible to catch. They never lose momentum. Some look like stars at first, others – blink and you'll miss 'em. Sure she'll leave at her leisure..." He held a baby carrot between two fingers like a rocket and glided it away from his body far as he could reach, then curved his trajectory and started pulling it back in. "But they're always guaranteed to circle back." He tipped the carrot towards her, before biting it and walking away. He severed the aggressive advances of his cousin Nick, who could use a break from chasing tail anyway. Shooed him away and insisted it was time to leave. Time, as he so colorfully illustrated, was of the essence.

Vertigo

His neck was really starting to hurt. His arm had been asleep for near of an hour. But so had she and he needn't dare move. Her gentle steady breathing passed casually in and out of snore. He heard music as he looked at her, though there was none playing. A beautiful melody from some enchanted land. They were back in full force and it must have worn her out. Eyes fluttering, she breathed heavy stirring awake, put off by brightness of room. Impromptu nap left shade open. Adjusting her hair behind ear so it wouldn't fall into her face, he kissed her forehead. Covered only in a blanket on a large white couch and though never cold, she pushed herself as close to him as she could as if she were.

The heat trapped in the blanket began to escape when she moved and he pulled the blanket up to keep it in. This weekend was just what they needed to get back in rhythm with one another. Then she shifted so her back was flat to his chest. Head rest over his left shoulder, face turned towards his neck. He wrapped his arms around her stomach, cheek to cheek with his sweet embraceable, as she folded hers over her blanket-covered breasts. Here it came. The part where he couldn't be satisfied. The part where he talked too much.

Pressing luck and ruining moments were two of his absolute specialties. All she wanted to do was wake up in his arms. In peace. Even laying on the couch they couldn't hold a cease fire. When he asked what she was doing the following weekend, she didn't answer right away. When she finally did, it wasn't the answer for which he was looking. He got dizzy. It felt like his legs were being pulled down into the depths, while he was to stay barely afloat. As she brought up Jan, he brought up Alex. Sick to his stomach, he couldn't even look down at her. She was too flush and dizzy to look up at him lest she fall right off the couch. Such a dizzying height.

They had climbed up there for a reason. Way up on that couch. The same reason aviophobes fly and thalassophobes swim. Because it takes three days to get from New York to LA by train. And because it takes a splash to get wet. The paralyzation began with the feeling he had when it was obvious whomever the Flyers were playing had sped down the ice and were about to score. He took a sharp turn back to the feeling he used to get so many years ago in school when the teacher would instruct the room to put their books away and there was a test for which he had forgotten to study. Quickly followed by the feeling one gets when being diagnosed with a terminal disease.

It broke after an eternity. He didn't want to wait in vain any longer. Now on opposite sides of the room, corner-to-corner, toe-to-toe, neither was yet ready to stop running from the inescapable. And it was set so that he was to take the heat. Good game played, burned again.

Cosmic Variance

Her neck was really starting to hurt. She had ditched the landscapes she was familiar with to check out some modern art. Which, the more years passed, the less sense it made to her. Neck would crane no longer attempting to see the beauty in this one. Back to killing time with Cole, Church. Church, ahh. She forgot to go that morning. All the hassle to get ready for this premiere exclusive luncheon gala kicking off in 20 and it slipped her mind it was Sunday.

Just as well. Mass had lost its charm in recent months.

She wasn't even sure why she was there. The artists would be ok. French impressionists, Monet, Cobot, Cezanne. It's that crowd. That bougie aristocracy that knows better than anyone how to suck the air clean out of the room. When hands reached high noon, the vacuum would be so tight someone couldn't rip a fart without their ass imploding. She had to get out of there. Her ass was way too fine to have old lady lipstick and old man mouth corner lip crust all over it. Too much flare in this star to waste another second pretending she knew which 't's' to pronounce or avoiding the bleeding worship of sycophants. Out she went.

Out to a beautiful day, this lonely star, struck with view, pulled out her camera. Past the roundabout and right down the street, her viewfinder offered all kinds of options. And with stunning detail. Had she been a sniper she could have picked off any target. Had she looked three centimeters to the right she would have seen him.

Less than a mile away, Meg Kelly was taking her smoke break. She always appealed to him. Her bitter disposition and misanthropic leanings made him wish she wasn't a lesbian. He swung by Il Saggiatore, not for the calamari or mozz sticks, but to see if his old friend could hook him up with some pain-killers. As always, she didn't disappoint, in company or supply.

"It's bullshit, dude." Slamming a handshake heartier than most of the men he knew could, she passed off 120 mg of Vicodin. "Like, you can't give me five days?" Her landlord was hitting her with a late fee for overdue rent. Slow week at the restaurant, the money he slipped her would make rent whole and fee covered. Jets remained uncool.

As she ranted and raved he leaned back beneath "E Pur Si Muove," one of dozens of nonsensical Italian signs posted around the building, he lit a cig-arette she bummed him. Added bonus in the sale. "No discount for dykes?" She punched him in the arm. Hard. "Ah," he rubbed it with his free hand. "Who taught you that word?" He breathed in through his teeth. "You did, ya dumb bitch." She laughed. "Who taught you to hit, Muhammad Ali?" "I wish," she took another drag. "I'd knock your ass out."

Listening pleasantly to threat, he stared up the street at the museum. A distant twinkling light made him look twice before he was startled back into coherence.

A car jumped the curb. Missed them by a mile, but scared the unholies out of them. "Jesus," Meg exclaimed. The driver, Patrick Lance, adjusted quickly and plopped back down onto the road in a flash. Unable to focus, Pat caught the sight of a smoking hot redhead in his rearview and couldn't take his eyes off. "Damn," Meg pointed her out to him, "I would crash too." He whistled to himself. The redhead was walking with her significantly shorter boyfriend, Kim Ho and would likely cause more accidents before the day was through. "What the hell is she doing with that Asian midget?" Meg griped. "Asian midget?" He was quick with the draw. "Isn't that redundant?"

"She could have anyone in the city," she ignored his quip. "She must see something in him," he offered. "I'm taller than he is," she grumbled. "You still with that weather chick?" Right in the sore spot. He shook his head. "Haven't heard from her in-" he trailed. "Whatta, ya got termination shock? Haven't accepted it's over? Gotta bow out sometime. Shame. Always seemed real with you. I can't watch her when she's on TV, makes me sick. Should win an award." His silence persisted for several moments as he dragged twice. "Or one for the role she played with me." Meg laughed. "They don't give Oscars for porn, buddy." She flicked the butt near the fresh tire mark on the curb. He followed suit and lifted his head. "They don't have to," he pounded her fist as she turned to go back to work. "Porn has its own awards."

Persona Non Grata

He couldn't stand the thought of hearing her defended again. He had told them next to nothing. She had told them everything. And then some. Friends' opinions mattered so little to him to begin with. Now even less so. Date night would be a much safer idea.

Jem Diamond was a stunning woman. The kind that drove every other man in a pub or club crazy. She was exactly his type. Tattooed. Pierced. Pixie cut, shaved on one side. Short. Smart. Flexible. The kind he could focus on and not be distracted by anyone walking by his table to use the bathroom. She was in the bathroom when he ordered their drinks. He had no idea what she wanted to eat. Or if she was even going to. She might have been one of 'those.' In which case she absolutely was not his type.

She didn't know anyone. What a treat. The city had gotten smaller and smaller over the years. Seldom did he meet anyone who didn't know someone who knows someone who knows someone who knows someone who.

His heart sank upon her return. He had forgotten himself and for the moment forgotten whom he was with. Only an idiot would be disappointed at the sight. She had the biggest eyes. Eyes that clearly adored him. To the point where both the man who sold him the rose now in her hair and the maitre'd who greeted and sat them felt the pressing impulse to comment on the matter.

The last time a stranger commented on the woman he was with, it made his night. This time it just upset him.

He wasn't rude. Not entirely engaging, but not rude. At the very least he needed to be hospitable. She was new here, her first time in the big city and he had to make a good impression. Reputation was a delicate matter for this metropolis.

Everything went well until she inquired about his personal life. She wasn't especially well read or versed in his end of popular culture, so she knew little of it. On the plus side, it meant he could disclose as he pleased. He wasn't there to do an interview. On the negative side, unlike his more recent interviewers, she didn't know which topics to avoid. Like all of them.

The fish was cooked to perfection, the libations were plenty, the atmosphere serene. But in an instant the conversation turned sour. She asked about his closest relations. Hadn't seen them in months. About his best friends. Down to one. And about his last relationship. Silence. He did his very best to deflect, but it was abundantly apparent the mood had surpassed its life expectancy.

When the question of dessert arose, the answer was clear to all parties involved. The waiter, Faulkner, lived down to his title and didn't wait for a verbal confirmation that he needed to print the check.

He paid. He felt terrible. He wanted to fix the situation, but it was no use. He would have paid anyway; the guilt merely propelled his hand to wallet.

Once closed out, he held the door for her and they were bum rushed with night air's sobering chill. She thanked him for a lovely time, told him she had fun, and insisted they do it again sometime. Lies one and all. Cab door opened for her, he administered the customary no one's getting any post date hug and sent her to her brand new apartment on the other side of town.

5 rtfm

The B Word

He sat thirsty as all hell in a rusted beach chair, here doubling as lawn furniture. Its support comprised of awful Teflon straps, a plaid pattern of faded green and orange with white lines along either side of each individual strap. Surely the product of secondhand acquisition, the chair did little to ease his discomfort in the matter. Strangling it by the neck, he raised the mouth of his Budweiser bottle to his and took a swig. The heatwave made quick work of its refreshing coolness and the second half of his third beer would have to be enjoyed lukewarm. It was, however, still cooler than his slow-burning forehead. Eyes closed, he pressed the bottle's body to his head, mixing beads of sweat with beads of condensation.

Dooley worked the grill. He was on his thirteenth Budweiser and didn't notice the shift of temperature. Well done was the only temp for this chef and the best anyone could hope for was that their burger have less charring than their neighbor's. Friends since high school, Dooley kept tradition alive by continuing to invite the gang over each summer or at least the part of the gang that hadn't come to despise each other. And the part that hadn't moved on via milestone. The Beef and Beers that originally served as reunions had long since dissipated. He had a beer gut now. Took years to cultivate and copious effort to maintain. Was going bald. That took no effort whatsoever. A true Irishman, he had a twinkle in his eye and brio in his wrist as he flipped burgers that were done eight minutes ago. What was left of his reddish blonde hair now contained traces of grey.

Dooley's wife, Crystal Dooley (nee Shepherd) was currently neglecting her sous chef responsibilities, which basically involved moving store bought potato salad from the fridge to the patio table, in exchange for several rounds of baggo. A relatively simple game, baggo involved trying to toss bean bags through a hole cut near the top of opposing boards slanted at roughly a 30° incline. Two teams of two would square off and try to outscore each other before they're too drunk to bear the weight of the bag.

He watched the Dooleys from his rusted throne. Clanking his rings to the side of the King Of Beers, his free hand pet the dog, Rex. He scratched his head beneath his Corona hat, sweat collecting on the brim. Legs folded, the bottle opener on his flip-flop looked more and more distant as the afternoon wore on.

Crystal looked to have a beer gut now too. A little extra weight behind the beanbag she was hurling and she was dominating the board.

The crowd was substantially denser than it had been the past several years. Due in part to people returning with toddlers turned prepubescent. One chased another past his feet as he gently volleyed a rock back and forth. He had come to, in no small way, really hate children and didn't bother hiding his laugh when one of them, Roger Fredrickson, Rog his parents called him, fell and hurt himself. Concern for Rog's well being left his inappropriate schadenfreude unnoticed.

But from the infantile and melodramatic squeals breaching eardrums from the boy who was more attention starved than hurt, his gaze was drawn beyond to a nightmarish oasis. There in the outer reaches of the backyard stood she. Pretty Girl.

The bottle dropped from his hand, spilling bubbly suds all over the dry grass. The rusted chair bore no root to hold it down and toppled back as he bolted up. Rage boiled over as he planned his next move. He looked on as they stood casually chatting with the friend of a friend who invited her new boyfriend. And she showed. To *his* reunion.

He started to charge, then balked. What would he say. Nothing. What, was he going to talk her out of the backyard, berate her until he embarrassed himself into having to leave? So he went the other way. Practically backflipped and was barreling towards the back gate, swatting past bumblebees and other bugs. Then BANG. He jumped. An explosion was the only thing that could have made him turn around. Behind him a blue nebulous cloud bellowed over the picnic table, benches and barbecue grill, lightly dusting the spread.

Crystal and Dooley, a couple endured since high school through the same will of not dying alone that beat in the hearts of every other mutant couple there who had stayed together since, were posed before the thick of it, arms outstretched. The moment wasn't awful enough, there had to be a gender reveal.

Suddenly, two more explosions. One pink. Another blue. Looks like the treatments had worked well. Too well. All began to clap boisterously, except one. Even her. Clapping for the unborn of a couple she didn't even know. The lone non-clapper lifted the bell shaped fork latch and let himself out through the postern. Bidding a true and hearty Irish goodbye to several dozen people he would never see again.

Gravity

Clicking on the radio he scanned with torpor through station after station to find something to listen to as salmon sizzled and rice steamed. He convinced himself it was for music and not to hear himself talk. Far too lame was the guy at this or any point in career who would go out of his way to experience his own work, let alone listen to a bore-ass interview. One where he copped out no less. The question was lobbed. Rachel Clark, experienced journalist and broadcasting personality, asked what it was like to work on the project. Rather than talk about what the experience really meant, how he had to delve deep for this one, for the church scene with the gun. How what he wrote for the hospital bed scene mirrored a profound experience with a dying relative. Et cetera. Instead it was idiot fodder. Experience was great. Other writers were great. Everything was great.

The actual answer was a bit more inclement. As he fiddled between adult contemporary and classic rock, he asked himself. What was it like working on that project? He answered. "Imagine there's a voice in your head. A person as real as anyone you know. You don't know them, but boy, do they know you. They know everything about you. And they're telling your story to the world. At first you're ok with it. Pleasant stroll down Memory Lane. But then they start into rooms and chambers and dusty halls you closed off and buried long ago. And hoped would remain closed. Long forgotten. And you beg and plead. 'Don't. Please don't. Please don't give them this.' Only to hear the voice of what is essentially a stranger whisper back, 'I have to.'" His fingers had rolled their way to NPR and Rachel Clark was reading him his life story abridged.

Over the years he had developed the most peculiar habit. It started out innocently enough. He would walk into the kitchen or his bedroom and wonder aloud, "Wait, why did I come in here?"

Something familiar to anyone, old or young. His inner thoughts would scramble until they uncovered the solution. "To get my glasses." Simple flub. Honest mistake. First person. But as time wore, the habit intensified. And with no one there to correct him, it never felt strange. "Why do I need my coat?" "Cold front came in." "Did I get my mail?" "Yes, I grabbed it earlier. Just junk. Again. As always." Then it started taking turns. "Do… you have to keep tapping that damn pen?" Or when he was sitting in traffic. "Why the hell did you go this way. You know better." A moment passed. "Because there's construction on 95, you idiot."

While the habit seemed disconcerting for anyone in the adjoining cars who watched his mouth move, but saw no passenger, it was one that may have behooved him to develop sooner. It's not that he wasn't self-aware, quite the contrary. Knowing when he was wrong or unusual was rarely the issue. Every once in a while he would find himself in a situation where the facts were stacked against and the odds bore no favor. And the voice in his head begged the case, pleading. "Please don't. Don't do this." And if he only ever learned to invert his giant fucking ears and listen. That if just once he had kept his mouth shut, then maybe he could learn to be happy once more.

Dying hard, some habits are impossible to rid. So as he switched his fork with his knife he stopped himself, asking aloud, "Why did you just do that?"

A moment passed. "Because you love her." Then he salted and peppered his previously frozen salmon filet, making sure to toss some salt over his right shoulder as he did. His chin retracted to his neck and wrinkles added to his brow. "Why did you just do *that*?" Another moment. "Because you miss her." A final drop of salt fell to salmon as he ate in humbled silence.

Lex Talionis

She called around 2:20AM. She knew he'd be up. Neither slept. He knew upon seeing it that something was wrong. She had drunk called him in the past, typically on her way home. He'd wonder if her calling was some sort of conciliatory effort to gain some favorable male attention on an evening where she struck out or if she actually just wanted to talk to him. A novel concept. Any of the calls would have come by 12:30AM or 1:00AM at the latest. This was different. She had called him two days prior and he had intentionally neglected to answer or return the call, a tactical he felt made him look more desirable. Girls who want to talk constantly will avoid any man who offers to listen consistently.

He returned her call just before 2:45AM. The girl he had over, Lauren McCrossen, lying half asleep on his couch was in no delicate way informed that he was making this call and it would take a while. He promptly left the room. Priorities.

He would be hers if only she would call. The holidays were theirs and in this, the wee small hours, she had. He was ready. Convinced beyond a shadow he knew this was the call for which he had been waiting years. She wanted to get back together. She had to. Nothing else made sense. Maybe she wanted to come over. He had to start conspiring. Had to get… what's-her-face out. Lauren. Ugh, why couldn't he remember that? He wasn't that drunk. Didn't matter. The moment was here. Not a second too soon. He was dying to go back to eating burgers and listening to sports talk radio. As God-awful as it could be, he missed it.

She was upset. And coked up. The deluge started promptly on the second ring. The information was scattered and mildly incoherent. Vague life crisis spilled in pieces here and there. He finger dusted the hall on his way to the back room. Only way he ever did. Strange that he detested the act so, yet refused to hire a service to clean. Dust was always an afterthought. At least he vacuumed.

It wasn't that he was bored. He was bored before she called. It was just the typical fare from her, nothing ever changed. He knew every word, but if you're going to a Buffett concert, you want to hear *Fins*. He wasn't going to interrupt.

It was on the third or fourth "I don't know what to do" where he was opening his mouth to invite her over. As he opened his mouth he heard a door shut.

"What was that?" There was no answer. Only the sound of a crackling fire. "Who's there?" he implored. The sound hadn't come from her, it was distant. Not a word. Not a sound. "Are you kidding me? You're still with Alex?" Finally, a response. "No." Rage filled him as her visitor made his way to his car, balls blued, sent into the cold, empty darkness, unaware that when he was asked to leave, he was supposed to do so surreptitiously. They flew into a fusillade of one awful slight after another, with he showing absolute zero concern if his guest was off put by denigrations. Feeling completely justified and embarrassingly sophomoric at the same time. The person to hang up first missed the final insult.

Fuming, he stood breathing hard and heavy in his kitchen. In his anger he had paced his way back. From there he could hear a theme song. Another episode of his favorite show had kicked off at the top of the hour. Never had such an eerie and unsettling tune brought such comfort. He was suddenly glad the chick in the living room was there. Tears hung out to dry, he returned without a word and led his guest by the hand up the stairs. He brought the woman he had no genuine intention of inviting to stay to bed. Meanwhile, the man whose green light had turned bright red drove his buzzed way home.

Any Consolation

Vince Wills could have gone pro in the NBA and was convinced the bartender needed to know about it. The pontificating didn't bother him nearly as much as the nature of the story. It was one of those half stories. A would have. A could have. That's not a story. No one wants to hear about how someone *almost* had something great. Actually played in the NBA. Yes. Couldn't play in the NBA because he had to go to war. Yes. Hell, he would have even settled for the time Vince Wills ran into Michael Jordan at a greater Chicago area Nike outlet. But this was nothing. 'Almost made it' doesn't count.

Three drinks deep and going strong, he had worked hard to drown Wills out. A concoction of his own creation did wonders for sore ears and tired heart. Fortunately, Almost Made It had cornered the bartender and was only occasionally redirecting when something needed special emphasis. Licking some serious wounds, he just wanted to be left alone and was certainly in no mood to humor.

The conversation started off pleasant enough. The windbag had finally given it a rest leaving room for someone else to chew his ears, a hearty feast to those who gab. The second act was considerably more appealing. He was now beholden his car service had mixed up the dates.

She wasn't waiting for a flight either. In fact, she had just come back on his, though her trip was to visit her sister. Conditions had not improved in her absence, she had found, as her husband told her when she landed that she could "just stay at the airport" and refused to make good on promised ride. Fine by her, the airport had bars and no lying snake in the grass scumbag lawyer husbands. At least none that she knew. The empty chair next to the familiar face from Row 4 Seat F seemed as good as any for pulling up.

"Waiting for a connection?" she excelled at openers. "I'd say I just made one," hand outstretched, he excelled at quick-witted replies. They shook and not that he needed to, but he beckoned her to join.

He ordered another whiskey ginger with a dash of elderflower, spot of aromatic bitters and a splash of lime juice, Irish Champagne as he called it, as she ordered a more traditional rum and Coke with a wedge. His drink name gave her a good laugh. Her observation that they were the only two in the city drinking at an airport bar with nowhere to go gave him a laugh equally needed. Half-listening when she gave her name, he began to offer his until she cut him short. It wasn't just from the plane that she recognized him. "You caught my eye… I read an article on you in the New Yorker a month or two ago. 'The Diagnostic Editor.' You're quite the big deal." He scoffed. "Depends on whom you ask." He sipped his 'champagne.' "Sometimes it doesn't matter how good you are, they hate you anyway."

"Well I was pretty bowled over," she insisted. "You've worked on three of my favorite movies."

"Out of 100?" he jested. "Out of 10," she flirted and they raised their glasses. They talked a great while. Rationalizing at his best, he tried to explain why drinking and writing were symbiotic. He quoted Oscar Wilde and Oliver Goldsmith much to her impress. She teased him and the bartender, at one point begging the bartender, Mack, to whip up some Jell-O shots. Light bulb on. That reminded him.

"Remind me to make a phone call when we get home." Rather presumptuous. Yet she neither argued nor questioned.

Mack kept flipping around on the TV. It was Saturday, so there were a lot of movies on. *Alien* on the science fiction network. *Pinocchio* on the Disney channel. *Bruce Almighty* on the comedy network. *Patton* on the history channel. *Breakfast At Tiffany's* on the classic film station. Unable or unwilling to pick a show, and ignoring his comments, Mack put the local news on. Ball game wasn't on until later and company policy didn't really allow movies to be played anyway.

The question of whether they should do another round arose. Scratch that. The decision was to not do another round. That had already been decided. The question if they should continue paying airport prices was on the board. As he mulled it over, beacon of broadcasting and head anchor, Cecily Allicott, turned it over to weather for the 5-day.

Last he spoke to her, she hadn't come to a clear decision regarding whether she was going back to her part time gig. It appeared she had made a choice in his absence. Two actually.

Remaining part of the most trusted meteorologists in the city was a bit more of a challenge. As she pointed at temperatures and cloud patterns, she was continually forced to adjust her position for the sake of visibility of those at home, while her other arm lay rest.

He did some quick math, lips moving while he did, as he stared at the bump. Not his. Not by a long shot.

With plenty of distraction and scarcely any time, he had yet to process what he saw on his way to the lecture the day before in that small café. Now he was half standing over a stool in an airport bar with what was left of his whiskey diluting by what was left of his ice. He was no longer doing math, but his mouth stay open. The feel of a hand placed on his shoulder snapped him back enough to close it. But not to break his gaze. Saliva rushed to his mouth over and over, almost faster than he could swallow it in his battle with the urge to throw up. There would be no rapprochement.

"Hey, you alright?" The voice sounded like it was in another terminal. He looked over. She saw weakness in his eyes, but no tears. Not today. "Let's get out of here," his voice was cracked, but not broken. Not today. Not yet anyway. "I'll grab my purse," she reached for it as he signed the credit card slip. All drinks on him. Then he realized he had to ask now, lest he find himself later in a situation he had put himself in a few times before. "Hey sorry," he stopped her. "What was your name again?" She smiled, not nearly insulted enough to not still go home with him.

"Gillian. But my friends call me… Gillian." He laughed softly as, with no attempt at grace, she swung her purse around her shoulder. Then they went down to baggage claim to hail a cab.

Daylight

The meal was proving a great success. Each bite better than the last. Candles lit, tree aglow in the corner. Bittersweet as their true beauty was to only be enjoyed by he. For when the daylight leaves, she would have to go. She was so grateful. He had even set the silverware on the proper sides etiquette wise. Only two settings for now, yet he had some hope. Never a firm desire for him before her, timing or age ever burdens. It was not a thought for her either, she dread the thought and even with the man she loved wasn't really up for ruining figure. Which also meant no dessert, the butter used would be the limit of the lactose she was willing to tolerate. But he knew her well. His mission was to change her mind. She had so much love, so much life force to give. And it was so apparent to him that her life force, her love would burn out eventually as all things do. Even if it took multiple lifetimes. It made no difference. His was here and now. She was so lovely. It was true for them both that love was indeed lovelier the second time around.

He loved how small her mouth would get when she chewed. He loved how she couldn't salt anything without tossing a dash superstitiously over the wrong shoulder. He loved how she had once again taken casual Friday too seriously and worn flip-flops with jeans. Rest assured he began teasing her the second she got to the top of the stairs. The way she wore her hat. The way her smile just beamed. The way she held her knife. Once sat and eating, he considered rehashing the issue of adding place settings, but settled instead for rehashing the issue of another trip. Their long weekend in the Windy City provided fine dining and escapism, precisely what they needed. He thought maybe once again he would pitch the idea of a long weekend to the Birthplace of Rock'n'Roll to party on Beale; something he hadn't anticipated would be such a difficult sell. Especially since, like their previous destination, it was a place neither had ever been. They chewed politely and stared at one another. Not in the way so many couples do, with years between them and nothing left to say. Rather with no words need spoken. The music, classical, her favorite, kept the mood light. At least for a time.

The argument got pretty heated. Minutes past no words and there were several, none too savory. It was over something stupid. They always were. She was so insistent. It made no sense. The sun had to be closer to the Earth during summer. Or Earth to the sun. Whatever. It had to. How else could he explain the seasons? Once again he was deflecting rather than offering facts, opting instead for personal attacks in the form of how she could possibly have missed that class with her impressive degrees. And the minor fact that she was a popular meteorologist. The phrase 'occupational hazard' was repeated ad nauseam. "How" she yelled indignantly, "how does that make sense?"

Nostrils flaring, he caught himself. His inclination to return blows was all of a sudden overcome with cool collection. She was so hot when she was mad. Fire in her eyes. He wiped his mouth with his napkin no longer in his lap and placed it on the table over his silverware. His chair scooched back, he stood and put his hands on the table. "Stand up," he commanded. Fire subsided to confusion and she glared not knowing what to expect. The command itself carried an air of impending pugilism, while his tone affirmed anything but. "Stand up," he repeated, an octave higher. She did as told.

Head tilted when cocked, she too placed her hands on the table in mocking fashion. Scoffing laugh shot from his nose. Smiling confidently, he beckoned her.

Resolute in her stand, it would take a second attempt. Still smiling, he insisted. "Come here." There was that voice she couldn't resist. Over she went. They stood face to face for a moment. She wanted to smile after a bit, but would never give him the satisfaction. Until she slipped. Holding out paid off and now he was free to move about without tension. "Ok think of it this way." He placed his hands around her forearms and at this proximity a different tension arose. He buried his eyes in hers. "Imagine" he breathed for effect, "my affection for you is the heat stabilized in the Earth's atmosphere." Smile sustained once more. He started to spin around at a steady pace. She looked at him as if he were nuts. Every time he would complete rotation he would look right at her, but only as he turned and soon his back was to her once more. She was confused. Right before she could utter 'what the hell are you doing,' and right as Holst switched to Debussy, he had stopped and was facing her directly once more. Now he took ten paces backward.

"Ok?" he poked. She shrugged, yet to catch on. "Now," he said and began spinning at the same pace. "I'm a million miles away. Or whatever." When he spun in this fashion again, he did the same and stared at her whenever they were facing. And as he did, her expression softened. Still spinning, he spoke. "As you can see, same pace. Respective sizes haven't changed. Though my orbit places me farther away, it gives me more time to look at you. With more time to look at you, my heart beats faster with every second. Each additional second of faster beating heart means greater love for you."

Her bottom lip was doing that thing. Where it sticks out and trembles because that dumbass jerk is being sweet again. She didn't speak. "Do you get it now?" Only nodded. He smiled and without ever even thinking the words 'I told you so,' he raised his arms to half-mast. This command need not be repeated and she came over into his arms. *Clair De Lune* floated mystically into the air as it always does and he took step in time. An appropriate serenade as it was the only way they could ever share it. The sound of music was no longer merely setting mood, it was conducting hearts and feet. She remained relatively still, right side of face pressed firmly to unpressed button down shirt. And he spun slowly around her.

PART V

Sunday Morning

Across a gravel parking lot adjacent to Surf Avenue was a small side street, Ocean Avenue. It had earned the name in the early days of the town's formation when it was a significant thoroughfare as it was always the first to flood when storms wreaked havoc. Years ago the top of the street was cut off in execution of a half-baked plan to divert flooding to newly installed storm drains and eventually the avenue turned to gravel as well. At the bottom of the street that could only be reached by cutting across the lot, property to the historic Majestic Hotel, was a uniformly historic house. One of a few remaining on the whole island, the old wooden house had seen its share of hurricane seasons and stood the test of ever increasing over development. Sandwiched between hotel and candy store. The Majestic, whose historic charm was so encompassing, guests checking in felt as though they had actually travelled back in time to a Prohibition Era of strong drinks and long smokes. Of loose women and scoundrels ready to oblige. And a quaint privately owned candy shoppe, Lichman's Sweets, boasting delicious homemade fudge and the best saltwater taffy in town.

Coming off the boards, Maria Ferreira finished her morning run by slowing to a walk coming around Lichman's. The tall, well-endowed brunette did not take the same notice of the porch that early gawkers took of her in her spandex. Notice was given to the wooden decorative post carved in the shape of a Native American's face. The original owners had it made and no resident had ever bothered or wanted to move it. Standing about seven feet tall, complete with traditional chief headdress, perhaps the most impressive things about the ligneous idol were those that sat atop.

Countless seagulls had perched tail feathers on wooden ones and yet neither Maria, nor any other passerby had ever noted an ounce of birdshit on or near the chief. As far as they or the current resident were aware, no bird had ever dared. Miniature onyx marbles in light brown freckled head stared blankly at her past sharp beak with black stripe and joined his tribal ancestors by not defecating on hallowed totem.

The show of respect went unobserved as she admired paneling and shudders. Shudders painted sea green swung loosely in the sea breeze with latches rusted loose. She listened to the clap against the walls, wiping the sweat off her brow with part of her top. She jogged in place for a moment, nodded towards a beautiful late middle-aged woman on her way to get bagels. Then continued her run. Even the late middle-aged woman going for breakfast stopped to gawk for a moment before consciousness of self took over and she hurried on her way.

Caribbean Blue

They awoke shortly after sunrise, as they usually did. It was his job to get the coffee and bagels. A new coffee shop had opened in Montego Bay Shopping Center eight blocks from their house. The barista was a 24-year-old Cuban expatriate named Ramondo who poured coffee in the morning, body built during the day, and watched the nightclub door at Eye Of The Hurricane at night. A fresh cut lay across his lower right cheek from a dramatic altercation the week before, adding an unneeded, but intensely welcomed, note of danger to his image.

Every time they'd been in there together he'd noticed her observing Ramondo's every move. Laughing at jokes told in broken English that neither one of them quite understood. Ramondo would Hispanically flirt irresistibly familiar. But because it was his job to get the bagels, her visits with Ramondo were few and far between, reserved specifically for days when they both had to be somewhere early. Weddings. Funerals. Day trips and do overs. Adventures and excursions. Odysseys and quests.

The only surprise when she offered to get them on this particular Sunday was that it took that many weeks to finally do so. He kindly kept all comments to himself and simply nodded and told her that would be great. She slid her freshly painted toes into her flip-flops and sauntered oh so gently out the door, leaving a single raised eyebrow in her wake.

His cut was healing nicely, but much to her delight, looked as if it would leave a scar. His complexion was not the best. There were divots here and there. But he made it work. And like the fresh fish in the marina, her breath had to be caught. The bell rang as the door closed and she placed her order. Odor of thick smoked hickory bacon loomed and while she made pleasant conversation over sound of sizzle with her apron-donned crush, she began to have second thoughts about her order. Bacon, egg and cheese on an everything? Freshly squeezed into tight fitting jeans, she wanted him to notice. But not notice *too* much. Should have gotten low fat cream cheese on plain. What if that jogger eats bagels to carb load? The moment passed and as she watched him bag it up with those rugged beige meat hooks he called hands, she began to feel confident again. "Thank you Ramondo," she said as innocently as she could muster. "De nada, ma'am."

It really hit her when she saw that old house again. Dozens of times she had been called that, taking it as complimentary. Sounded distinguished. She was in such a daze that nothing seemed out of the ordinary as she circled round back. Wasn't until she was coming around the outdoor fenced in shower owner and guests used to wash off sand coming off the beach that she snapped out of it. "Crater face," she mumbled. The comment lay snuggly under breath. The deep calming blue of the exterior was placating. A shade that had it appeared in any non-resort town would have induced instantaneous melancholia. But such potentially gloomy colors here were ubiquitous and very welcomed. She supposed she could forgive him for just one silly insignificant slight.

The Holly And The Ivy

She tripped on the gravel and partially spilled one of the coffees. That one can be his, she thought. A heavy whiff of salt air on a mild breeze temporarily masked the aroma of fresh roasted bean. It also blew hair to face and she almost tripped a second time. Lived at the beach for years now and still couldn't adjust to open toed footwear. The gravel had scratched chips of purple paint off a few toes. She would have to do them over.

Sloshing through a puddle of dirty beach with God knows what in it she began to resent him. Sitting at home, in magnificent desolation, reading the news in his favorite recliner with the sound of the morning surf bringing the tide in and punctual birds making personal caws. She was more than willing to generously overlook the fact that it was her idea. Ramondo, that stupid sexy jerk.

As she cornered the Caribbean Blue façade, a glaring flash of green caught her eye. Be it angle or routine, she had never noticed it before. On their Sunday walk they would often speak with the old timer who lived there, usually out in his Sunday finest, sweeping the porch of sand with an old witch's broom. He must have distracted her. As she came around, more green.

Uncommon for the region, but not uncommon for a building that old, hefty vines of ivy had climbed to the roof. Stranger still, beneath them lie a very round, very lush, very out of season, holly bush. Shades that, had they appeared in any non-resort town, would have appeared completely natural.

Bright red berries blazing through pointy defenders put a song in her head. The words were all wrong though. Hearing through the ears of her better half, she was relatively certain the original crooner never made sexual innuendo of 'chestnuts roasting on an open fire' or 'Jack Frost nipping.' Then she laughed. She was as bad as he was. Her amusement was abruptly interrupted by a scratchy pain in her feet as several holly leaves found their way into her flops.

When she got home, he got yelled at. Looking up from the news through the tops of his glasses, he witnessed her slam the coffee and drop the sandwich bag on the island. Lips pulled in and head turned to the side with furrowed brow as she yelled, "Next time, you're going." Then proceeded to shrug it off to the fairer he had given up trying to figure out long ago.

Dark Skies

They held hands as they walked down the eastern shore's golden sands. Close enough to the shoreline for their toes to catch waves' end. A large brown seagull resting a few yards away was incensed with the need to yell in their ears as they walked by. The obnoxious cry was home to them. A lone sailboat drift aimlessly a few leagues out, sails down, ambling southward. The denizen of the vessel were in no rush. A slight haze wrapped the horizon creating a minor decrease in visibility on this otherwise cloudless day. The weatherman had called for a possible shower late afternoon and though the day was still in its infancy, no foreseeable credibility was lent to his prediction. The biplanes had yet to begin their runs, advertising AUCE crabs and eastern shore style fried chicken. No news yet on the day's happy hours. The parasailers had yet to begin their ascent to the heavens. The air was as fresh and the sky as clear as it would be all day.

They passed another couple, Pat and Cleo, half their age, perhaps on their first vacation together or even on their honeymoon following a late summer wedding. Labor Day was the perfect time to be at the beach. All the popular haunts were readying themselves for one last summer bash, while the kids were all back in school lamenting nine months of state capitals and the Pythagorean theorem, Christmas would be their only refuge from here till June and Santa couldn't come fast enough.

They must have wandered a bit too close to shorebreak, as an unusually large wave crashed on top them, knocking him over and soaking her legs. She readily found the humor in the situation and began laughing hysterically, though he was not so amused. Her joviality fueled his anger and his tirade opened with a good strong, "Oh, you think this is funny," and continued from there. Ever the gentleman, it was the rare instance, but he could be a real dick when he wanted to be. Much ado over some wet shorts and a damp wallet.

Walking resumed in awkward silence. Then freeze. Two things seemed strange in this otherwise mundane routine. One, the old man sat in his favorite chair wearing, not his Sunday best, but dressed still in his evening wear. A light blue cotton button down shirt with pants to match, his glasses on. Although that was no indication, he had never switched to contacts. Two, he didn't wave back.

They looked at one another, dead in track, realizing that something wasn't right. She looked down. She wanted to proceed, even reluctantly taking a few steps forward. He, ever her rock, gently grabbed her arm, encouraging her to follow him on their impending investigation.

The sun beginning to feel much hotter, they approached the porch as slowly as they could without feeling guilty for taking their time. Shorts were quick to dry and now the collected sand in his boxers was the least of his worries. He was moving slightly faster than she. He yelled the old man's name as they got within earshot. No response. The old man had told them on more than a few occasions that he was hard of hearing, so hope maintained. They quickened their pace. His skin color became progressively more palid as they approached and their pace increased once more. He yelled the old man's name, inquired if he was ok. No response. This time faulty hearing could not be blamed.

The Old Man's House

The weather worn steps of the back porch creaked and cracked as he climbed. She stood a few feet back, hands over mouth, accepting the reality of what was going on. He clasped the cold wrist, vainly searching for a pulse. He placed his hand under the nose. He was only going through the motions, he knew as well as Death did. She was crying now. What might be a meaningful tribute if it weren't fact that earlier in the week she had cried watching a late night commercial encouraging pet adoption. "Gina," he said with a clear break in his voice. "Call an ambulance."

She followed suit up the stairs to go into the house for a phone. The door was slightly ajar and as she shoved it open, she hesitated. "Derrick." She turned to face him, doing her best to position her stare so the corpse wouldn't be in her line of vision. She placed a hand on the receiver and froze. Realizing that given her state he had asked too much, he took her place and dialed. Although he wasn't entirely sure this constituted an emergency, he was relatively certain that 911 was protocol in this situation as well.

He began to dial, but before he could make it to the second 1 he noticed something. A piece of paper lay beneath the old man's left hand, a corner gently fluttering in the sea breeze. She caught him looking at it, but with the screen door and tears blocking her vision, she made her way back to see. She almost went for it before a wave of nausea swept over her rendering her stomachless to touch a dead body, even if it was a dear friend. Knowing she'd never make it, he stepped forward and respectfully removed the paper from the dead man's grip. Rigor mortis made this a more difficult task than it should have warranted, but after a few seconds of wriggling, the paper jarred free. It was a note. Folded once. As if discovering a buried treasure chest he opened it, not as a pirate would, slinging it open with ravenous delight at the plunders ready to be spent. But rather like an eminent archeologist, expectantly curious, but reverent of the fact that a small piece of history lay mercifully in his hands.

He read moving his lips as he did when he read anything. Normally this would be her cue to make fun of him. Here she did not. It was a brief note. He frowned puzzled, glanced at her then read it once more. A queer smile rose and he refolded it and placed it in his back pocket. "What did it say, Der?" He shook his head, moving back inside. "Really, what?" she insisted. "I'll tell you later," he defied. Sadness soon overwhelmed once more and the idea moved to the back of her mind.

The wait for the ambulance was long. He had of course told them not to rush. They sat in silent vigil in the old man's living room. For a fleeting moment Derrick considered turning on the TV or even the radio, but nothing aired would likely be relevant. He stood and began to peruse. Several items caught his eye. There was the room's centerpiece, a large model wooden ship. A three masted Spanish Galleon, *The Rose Marie,* handcrafted and decades weathered. She was yar. Very yar indeed. Very fitting for the living room of a beach house. The flip-flops by the door with the bottle opener built in. He laughed. Turning to Gina to share the amusement, he noticed her green complexion. Seasick on shore. "Would you like a soda?" She nodded. "I'll check the fridge." He made his way to the kitchen nearly tripping over a large black Frisbee. "We can use his flip-flops to open it." He opened the door.

He paused a moment when he noticed a Christmas card held to door by way of Key West magnet. Odd it would still be up given the time of year. Also odd given the only other thing on there was a deli menu. Odder still as the reds and golds had faded suggesting it wasn't from the previous Christmas.

A true bachelor. Half a hoagie, beer, some mustard, and dessert. Bowl full of Jell-O. No help there. As he closed it, he spotted a bottle of Ginger Ale on the door's shelf. Bingo.

True to his word, he cracked it open with footwear and served. The idea that there was one degree separating her soft drink to an old man's foot didn't seem to slow her down. She took a huge swig. In an instant a follow up swig had settled her stomach and soothed her nerves.

Lady she was, she passed the bottle and he followed suit. With her hands freed she rummaged through a pile of books on the coffee table. An old one caught her eye. Hardback. One of the few titles she recognized. It was a classic, she had read it in high school. She opened it and before reading the inscription, pressed it to her nose and breathed deep. Old book smell. She was right back in the library. As the dust settled in her lungs, she read.

"To My Pretty Girl, if ever you feel lost, read this and think of me. For I was lost and you were there to light my way back. My Love Forever Yours-"

Afraid the returning tears would run the ink, she pulled back. Before closing, she kissed the tip of her middle finger and pressed it to his signature. Then placing the book back on top of the pile, he stopped her. "Keep it." She was so unsure. "Oh I couldn't" she countered. "No really," he picked it up and placed it in her lap. "We both know no one else is getting it. He'd want you to." After a considerable amount of humming and hauling, she consented.

"Who could that have been?" "You don't think he was pretty?" he quipped. She laughed through sobs and heaves. "What if she rejected him?" she worried. He thought for a moment. "Or if she gave it back to him?" He thought a second more. "Maybe it ended before he had a chance to give it to her" he comforted. "And never had the heart to let it go." "The last girl he ever loved?" She pondered. The question was haunting in a sense. "Maybe just the best." They were both right. And both wrong. The man who sat peacefully outside had lived a full and vibrant life. The list of characters he had the pleasure and displeasure of getting involved with read like a list of Disney sidekicks or Dick Tracy villains or rejected rapper stage names.

Boo Sneeze. Sweetheart. Vicki Skullz. Tricky Baby. DC. Platform Girl. Big Mac. Mickey D's. Natali With No E. Math Girl. Big Red. Bubbles. Short

Round. Giggles. Chuckles. The Mom. Double Dees. Pizza Hut. The French Tickler. Pretty Girl. Miller Time. Brown Out. The Indian. The Russian. Jilly Bean. Friz. Special K. Glowworm. E.T. Liv Tyler Has A Boyfriend. The Pastor. The Chilean. Meghan From Maine. Pepper. Umbrella Girl. African Queen. Rizzie. Barbie. Members Only. Franley. Strawberry Mansion. New York. EPCOT. The French Hornist. Princess. Mesh Shorts. Swanson. Judd. Jannellezabub. BC. Scotty. Almond Joy. Kitty Kat. The Nurse. Asshole. Psycho. Bells. Rocket. Jaws. The Other One. Road Runner. Housewife. Pickles. Scout. Stardust. The Waitress. Starbuck. Laura Powers. Thumper.

The ambulance arrived and Derrick had a few words with the EMTs before they came in to do the most unpleasant part of their job. She finished her Ginger Ale and placed the bottle back down. Then picked it up and moved it to a coaster just in case. As they left, they took one last look around and she tucked the book tightly against her hip as she closed the door behind her. She felt better now taking the book. She knew he wouldn't have minded. For the old man was kind.

Zikhrono Livrakha

There was no music playing. Dragging long bouts of silence. The pipe organ, almost as old as the church, sat quietly in requiem collecting dust while the town's only remaining organist was, funny enough, on vacation. Relief came only in the form of creaking wood from the few souls shifting in their pews. Wasn't like Father O'Malley to be late. He prided self on punctuality. Derrick and Gina walked in easing the heavy door shut behind them. Seated in the back, intent was to leave closer seats for closer relatives and friends. Once sat, they soon realized they were merely making elbowroom for the five or six there. "Is this it?" Derrick asked Gina. "Guess so," Gina answered.

He wandered over to the organ and fiddled with it, playing a few random notes. B flat. C. A flat. A flat, an octave down. E flat. Until Gina smacked his hand and murmured 'knock it off' through grinding teeth. He was only trying to help. The room was sepulchral, musty, doleful, funereal. Even for a room hosting a funeral. In walked Father O'Malley. That was odd. If they weren't waiting for him, then what.

In walked an older woman who immediately began scanning the room. Her eyes fell upon another old woman already sitting. She went to join the woman who when seeing her at pew's end jumped up to greet a friend not seen in ages. They sat close to the front, three pews back, holding hands. The reunion was sobering. Likely the last of the attendees. One leaned into the other to whisper something. Father O'Malley took the podium.

"Ladies and Gentlemen, thank you for joining us today. Our guest of honor is running late. Drawbridge is malfunctioning, the hearse is stuck." Son of a bitch. Everyone shifted uncomfortably in their seats and shared glances. "If there are no objections, I'll go ahead with eulogy and we'll commence the remainder of the mass when he arrives." There were no objections from the baker's dozen or so of personal favors currently present. Two there out of curiosity. Two there out of duty. The rest…

He started with the standard biographical information. Name, DOB, place, things, moves, relatives, yadda yadda yadda. Favorite TV Show: *Seinfeld*. Favorite food: Soft pretzels. Covered in crab dip. Favorite Beatle: George. Favorite flavor: Malt. Favorite Song: *In The Deep* by Bird York. Oldie but a goodie. Album: *Crazy Monsters And Super Creeps*. Even older. Animal: Turritopsis Dohrnii. Potentially ancient. Obligatory, but not the least bit interesting. "He had made a profitable living doing what he never wanted – other people's work. Became renowned in the industry as the man who could fix any book, any screenplay. He chose his work carefully and was compensated handsomely. A dramaturge is something of a diagnostic editor. A fitting vocation for the man able to help everyone, but himself. He did the heavy lifting, came up with the best ideas, while others harvested accolades. And we'll never know the true extent of the body of his work, as he was so prone to using nom de plumes. One of his best works, a novel about remorse and lamentation in a post-apocalyptic wasteland, won a Pulitzer Prize. The award sits proudly on a mantle thousands of miles from his home."

On he went really bringing the room down. Then he turned a corner and things got a bit lighter. "He often spoke of the women of his life." At least four perked up. "In fact, he seldom spoke of much else. The good and the bad. The great, the unforgettable. The awful, the imploding. The pull, the gravity. Gravity keeps us safe. The abyss is huge, vast, daunting. Even terrifying. As long as we're planted on the ground, we take no risk." He paused for dramatic effect. "But he wasn't one to avoid risk. He proposed once. She laughed and told him to get off the ground. Lived with a woman. It was court mandated. He went on a two-week vacation with a woman. She couldn't accept the prize otherwise. He met families. They didn't like him. He gave a girl a ring. It was a bottle opener. He bought a house with a woman. As a rental investment. He was part of a couple's Halloween costume. The rest of the group didn't show. He was engaged. Briefly. She needed citizenship." Laughter waned. The list was out anyway. Just in time for the old man's arrival.

Ouroboros

The mass concluded. He finished the eulogy strong, solid homily, traditional mass. Made sure to point out that it was an act of charity, the deceased was not the religious type. Another favor. When the two older women exited the church, both without blessing themselves, Derrick and Gina felt compelled to say something. They reacted more than anyone else and cried at various times. And Derrick was almost certain one was Pretty Girl. As they shook Father's hand and descended the steps, Derrick nudged Gina and nodded towards the woman he believed to be the book's proper owner, the one who was first to arrive.

Gina as awkward as ever, crept uneasily towards them. With no break in their ongoing conversation, she was forced to interrupt. Neither minded and one was quick to implore how she knew the deceased. Geezer who used to sweep his porch, tell long stories, and she was the one who found his corpse. She settled for addressing him as a casual acquaintance.

Nothing rehearsed, she didn't say much beyond that and lifted the book up to hand it to one of the women. Graciously taking it, his Sweetheart of old opened to the inscription and smiling with a tear passed it off to its rightful recipient. Derrick was close. 50/50 shot. The other woman whose radiance had survived to antiquity took the book and after blinking and pulling it back and forth to adjust her eyesight, read dutifully.

Her lips were doing that thing. That thing they hadn't done in years. Her heart had leapt higher than it had in decades. Along with it dissolved any question as to whether it was a good idea to go. She closed the book, not wanting to look again until she got home. As a thank you she only nodded. It was all she could muster. And all the interaction Gina wanted. Ready to cry herself, she ran back to Derrick with an overwhelming sense of accomplishment.

"I have a message of my own," Derrick was holding the note in his right hand, unsheathed from his suit pant pocket. The old man had a trick or two left up his sleeve. Derrick opened it with both hands for her to come around and read. She looked puzzled to him and he shrugged. "Sounds good to me," he affirmed as he slid the note commanding "Take Her For Ice Cream" into the breast pocket of his Sunday best.

Syzygy

A tuna salad sandwich with rippled chips was placed in front of Pretty Girl, while a large house salad with Thousand Island dressing was simultaneously placed in front of Sweetheart. And Gina- their waitress, not their mailwoman- asked if there was anything else they needed for now. They were good. Pretty

Girl sipped her root beer, a drink that never appealed to Sweetheart. She thought it tasted like bubblegum. But she liked bubblegum, a contradiction no one felt the need to shed light on. She was drinking an Arnold Palmer. They talked about a great many things between bites. Miles and miles to catch up on. Lunch was such a lovely idea. They were reminded soon in how much they used to enjoy one another's company.

Friends through a mutual acquaintance, their bond had historically been one more of convenience than anything else, though as they were realizing in the course of the late afternoon, they could have been friends regardless. They had a surprising number of common traits despite their differing race and upbringing. If felt delightfully natural. And here they thought they might have to force it.

At a certain point one asked the other why they hadn't done a better job staying in touch. The excuse was age old, they had let life get in the way. An attempt to return the conversation to more casual topics failed and before long they were speaking of regrets.

The inevitable took an uncomfortably long time to come up. Particularly given he was the reason they were there. Maybe it was their age and tendency to ramble. Maybe it was because he was so far back in the rearview, he was barely detectable. Maybe it was because neither wanted to admit that perhaps he was their greatest. Tough call. Sweetheart was happily married for years before her dearly beloved succumbed, Pretty Girl was contently herself for a lifetime. "He was a dear," Sweetheart reminisced. "He was my first kiss, you know." "I remember. Certainly wasn't mine." They shared a laugh to those foolish things. "But somehow, he felt like it." They both drank. No toast. Then the question neither wanted to ask. What happened. Now they knew why they didn't want to ask. Neither knew how to answer. The excuse that was promptly brought to mind was not one either was willing to use. They wouldn't dare cheapen their experience with him, not today. Somehow 'life got in the way' really wasn't going to cut it. He deserved better, even if it wasn't an option.

Pretty Girl paid, she had already gotten her gift for the day. She clenched her book close to her chest as they exited what was essentially a diner in the middle of the parking lot for a business unrelated. The salt air filled their tired old lungs and the gravel lot made walking even more of a chore than it already was. They didn't want to say goodbye and they didn't have to. New numbers exchanged, they vowed to do better. A promise they would both keep. A hug between old friends is always a sight, even if its just for seabirds overhead. Then Sweetheart said something Pretty Girl never expected.

"Thank you." The words almost got stuck in her throat. Pretty Girl didn't know what to make of it. It wasn't for lunch; she already thanked her for that. And it wasn't for the day. Thinking she had it figured out, she came close to asking, but decided against. Instead she nodded as she always did. No sense ruining a perfect moment on what was, all in all, a perfect day.

Scintillation

Why do stars twinkle? She asked observing one appearing near the horizon as the sun fell from the sky. "To get your attention," he answered half kidding, half not knowing. A man sitting with his wife at an adjacent bench scoffed audibly. An ironic condescension as he himself didn't know the answer either. "I wonder why the sky changes so many colors when the sun is setting," she mused aloud, further testing his knowledge of the cosmos. "I believe it's caused by the sun reflecting off the water," he answered incorrectly, having no earthly idea on the natural phenomenon known as scattering. Where light particles are forced to deviate from a straight trajectory by one or more paths due to localized non-uniformities in the medium through which they pass. "Like a rainbow. You ever watch Captain Noah growing up?" He did what he always did when he found himself painted into an intellectual corner. He brought up something faintly relevant in order to switch the subject to something better suiting his expertise. In this case, Children's Saturday Morning regional television programs. "Oh my God, yeah," she responded as if they hadn't had this conversation a dozen times before. "My parents had all these old recordings." "Yeah mine too. They would put the tapes in every Saturday morning to buy themselves an extra couple hours of sleep." This of course was proceeded with them singing, very much out of key, the forgotten lyrics to a song gone unbroadcasted for decades. Captain Noah, or W. Carter Meierbrier was a Philadelphia broadcasting pioneer who made his final airing in the mid 1990's and died nearly twenty years later. Too local for any kind of home video release, his memory hinged on the middle aged to elderly who could still recall waking up early in the Delaware Valley to check and see if the good Captain had selected their hand drawn artistic submissions to feature on his show. Their deharmonized tune ended in a fit of laughter nearly causing them to drop their treats. At that moment a rare sight, a shooting star in the fading light of day, streaked across their peripheral vision. "Make a wish," she commanded. "No need," he said as naturally as if he had rehearsed it all day. She desperately tried to hold back her smile, reluctant to give him credit, but it was no use. His corny charm got her every time. As her eyes lit up, magic hour kept alive just a wee longer.

They sat on that bench eating their dessert. With all the people crossing behind. So many couples. Some already passed, some yet to catch up. The depth of sonder flowed shallow for these two. Unbeknownst to them which couples set to stay together against better interest. Unable to ever admit that it just wasn't working. Neither brave enough to leap; too gutless to walk alone. Or all the couples who would come to fail. When they might have made it if either were willing to tuck some tail and admit they'd never survive without the other. All he knew, was the day was getting on. All she knew was her ice cream was melting fast. She giggled as she finished it and it dripped down her chin. He grabbed a napkin and manned clean up duty. Back to being a gentleman.

He continued down to brush sand off her toes, but she stopped him. A silly task trying to keep sand away at the beach, she pointed out. Where the grains of sand were outnumbered only by the stars in the sky. Then standing, in true gentleman form, he gave her a kiss and walked her home.